First World War
and Army of Occupation
War Diary
France, Belgium and Germany

1 INDIAN CAVALRY DIVISION
Divisional Troops
1 Indian Field Squadron Royal Engineers
2 February 1915 - 31 December 1916

WO95/1170/4

The Naval & Military Press Ltd
www.nmarchive.com
Published in association with The National Archives

Published by

The Naval & Military Press Ltd

Unit 10 Ridgewood Industrial Park,

Uckfield, East Sussex,

TN22 5QE England

Tel: +44 (0) 1825 749494

www.naval-military-press.com

www.nmarchive.com

This diary has been reprinted in facsimile from the original. Any imperfections are inevitably reproduced and the quality may fall short of modern type and cartographic standards.

© **Crown Copyright**
Images reproduced by permission of The National Archives, London, England, 2015.

Contents

Document type	Place/Title	Date From	Date To
Heading	WO95/1170/4		
Heading	BEF 1 Ind. Cav Div Troops 1 Ind. Fld Sqdn. R.E. 1915 To 1916 Dec		
Heading	War Diary of 1st Indian Field Squadron R.E. 1st Indian Cavalry Division. From 2nd February 1915 To 28th February 1915		
War Diary	Clarques	02/02/1915	07/02/1915
War Diary	St. Hilaire	08/02/1915	28/02/1915
Heading	War Diary of 1st Indian Field Squadron R.E. 1st Indian Cavalry Div From 1st March 1915 To 31st March 1915		
Heading	War Diary of 1st Indian Field Squadron RE 1st Indian Cavalry Division I. E. F. A. From 1st March 1915 To 31st March 1915		
War Diary		01/03/1915	15/03/1915
War Diary	Les Pesses	16/03/1915	18/03/1915
War Diary	Erny St Julien	19/03/1915	20/03/1915
War Diary	Serny	21/03/1915	31/03/1915
Heading	War Diary of 1st Indian Field Squadron RE 1st Indian Cavalry Div From 1st April 1915 To 30 April 1915		
War Diary	Serny	01/04/1915	30/04/1915
Heading	War Diary of 1st Indian Field Squadron RE From 1st May 1915 To 31st May 1915		
War Diary	Serny	01/05/1915	10/05/1915
War Diary	Wittes	11/05/1915	28/05/1915
Heading	Rubrouck	29/05/1915	31/05/1915
Heading	War Diary of 1st Indian Field Squadron RE From 1st June 1915 To 30th June 1915		
War Diary	Rubruck	01/06/1915	04/06/1915
War Diary	Near Branhoek	05/06/1915	07/06/1915
War Diary	Near Brandhoek	08/06/1915	13/06/1915
War Diary	Ypres	13/06/1915	15/06/1915
War Diary	Blamart	16/06/1915	30/06/1915
War Diary	Fosse	30/06/1915	30/06/1915
Heading	War Diary of 1st Indian Field Squadron From 1st July 1915 To 31st July 1915		
War Diary	Fosse	01/07/1915	31/07/1915
Heading	War Diary of 1st Indian Field Squadron RE 1st Indian Cavalry Division. From 1st August 1915 To 31st August 1915		
War Diary	Roquitoire	01/08/1915	31/08/1915
Heading	War Diary of 1st Indian Field Squadron RE From 1st September 1915 To 30th September 1915		
War Diary		01/09/1915	30/09/1915
Heading	War Diary of 1st Indian Field Squadron RE From 1st October 1915 To 31st October 1915		
War Diary		01/10/1915	15/10/1915
War Diary	Domart	16/10/1915	21/10/1915
Heading	Liomer	22/10/1915	31/10/1915
War Diary	War Diary of 1st Indian Field Squadron RE From 1st November 1915 To 30th November 1915		

War Diary	Liomer	01/11/1915	30/11/1915
Heading	War Diary of 1st Indian Field Sqn. R E November 1915		
Heading	War Diary of 1st Indian Field Squadron RE From 1st December 1915 To 31st December 1915		
War Diary	Liomer	01/12/1915	15/12/1915
War Diary	Embreville	16/12/1915	31/12/1915
Heading	War Diary of First Indian Field Sqn. R E First Indian Cav Divn Dec. 1915		
Heading	War Diary of 1st Indian Field Squadron RE From 1st January 1915 To 31st January 1916		
War Diary	Embreville	01/01/1916	31/01/1916
Heading	War Diary of 1st Indian Field Squadron RE From 1st February 1916 To 29th February 1916		
War Diary	Embreville	01/02/1916	29/02/1916
Heading	War Diary of 1st Indian Field Squadron, R E From 1st March 1916 To 31st March 1916		
War Diary	Embreville	01/03/1916	26/03/1916
War Diary	Oneux	27/03/1916	27/03/1916
War Diary	Auxi-Le-Chateau	28/03/1916	31/03/1916
Heading	War Diary of 1st Ind. Field Sqn RE 1st Ind Cav Divn March 1916		
Heading	War Diary of 1st Indian Field Squadron RE From 1st April 1916 To 30th April 1916		
War Diary	Auxi-Le-Chateau	01/04/1916	30/04/1916
Heading	War Diary 1st Indian Field Squadron RE 1st Ind. Cav. Divn April 1916		
Heading	War Diary of 1st Indian Field Squadron RE From 1st May 1916 To 31st May 1916		
War Diary	Hanchy	01/05/1916	05/05/1916
War Diary	Auxi-Le-Chateau	06/05/1916	10/05/1916
War Diary	Liencourt	11/05/1916	31/05/1916
Heading	War Diary of 1st Indian Field Squadron 1st Indian Cavalry Division May 1916		
Heading	War Diary of 1st Indian Field Squadron RE From 1st June 1916 To 30th June 1916		
War Diary	Liencourt	01/06/1916	29/06/1916
War Diary	Doullens	30/06/1916	30/06/1916
Heading	War Diary 1st Indian Field Squadron 1st Indian Cavalry Division June 1916		
Heading	War Diary of 1st Indian Field Squadron RE From 1st July 1916 To 31st July 1916		
War Diary	Doullens	01/07/1916	01/07/1916
War Diary	Auxi-Le-Chateau	02/07/1916	18/07/1916
War Diary	Agnieres	19/07/1916	31/07/1916
Heading	War Diary 1st Indian Field Squadron 1st Indian Cavalry Division July 1916		
Heading	War Diary of 1st Indian Field Squadron RE From 1st August 1916 To 31st August 1916		
War Diary	Agnieres	01/08/1916	31/08/1916
Heading	War Diary 1st Indian Field Squadron 1st Indian Cavalry Division August 1916		
Heading	War Diary of 1st Indian Field Squadron RE From 1st September 1916 To 30th September 1916		
War Diary	Agnieres	01/09/1916	02/09/1916
War Diary	Cantileux	03/09/1916	03/09/1916
War Diary	St Riquier	04/09/1916	10/09/1916

War Diary	Occoches	11/09/1916	11/09/1916
War Diary	Doulens	12/09/1916	12/09/1916
War Diary	Frechencourt	13/09/1916	14/09/1916
War Diary	Ville sur Ancre	15/09/1916	17/09/1916
War Diary	Fricourt	18/09/1916	26/09/1916
War Diary	Bussy Les Daours	27/09/1916	27/09/1916
War Diary	Picquigny	28/09/1916	28/09/1916
War Diary	Francieres	29/09/1916	29/09/1916
War Diary	Crecy Grange	30/09/1916	30/09/1916
Heading	War Diary of 1st Indian Field Squadron 1st Indian Cavalry Division September 1916		
Heading	War Diary of Field Squadron, 4th Cavalry Division (late 1st I.C. Divn) From 1st October 1916 To 30th November 1916		
War Diary	Crecy Grange	01/10/1916	15/10/1916
War Diary	Marcheville	16/10/1916	24/10/1916
War Diary	Boismont	25/10/1916	31/10/1916
Heading	War Diary 1st Indian Field Squadron 1st Indian Cavalry Division October 1916		
War Diary	Boismont	01/11/1916	30/11/1916
Heading	War Diary 4th Field Squadron 4th Cavalry Division November 1916		
Heading	War Diary of Field Squadron RE 4th Cavalry Division From 1st December 1916 To 31st December 1916		
War Diary	Boismont	01/12/1916	31/12/1916
Heading	War Diary 4th Field Squadron R.E., 4th Cavalry Division. Dec. 1916		

WO 95/11704

BEF

1 IND. CAV DIV
TROOPS

1 IND. FLD Sqd. R.E.

1915 FEB. to 1916 DEC

(Box 3303?)

Serial No 13.

WAR DIARY
OF

1st Indian Field Squadron, R.E., 1st Indian Cavalry Division.

From 2nd February 1915 To, 28th February 1915

WAR DIARY
or
INTELLIGENCE SUMMARY.
(Erase heading not required.)

Instructions regarding War Diaries and Intelligence Summaries are contained in F.S. Regs., Part II, and the Staff Manual respectively. Title pages will be prepared in manuscript.

No 3 Section
S Office at Base
I.F. Force
Passed by .... S. Sect[n]
on 4-3-15

Hour, Date, Place.	Summary of Events and Information.	Remarks and references to Appendices.
CLARQUES. 2-2-15	Indian R.E. Began taking over from O.C. 2nd Field Squadron the following detachment 1st Indian Field Squadron R.E.- 1 " Driver Sergt R.E. 1 " Corpl " 3 " Lce. Corpl " 51 Drivers R.E. 20 Vehicles 103 horses	
3-2-15 to 5-2-15	and a small percentage of equipment. Taking over stores and kicking manege, harness, colours & cliquifs Cars, carry horses. One shifted from lives suffering with lice. On 5-2-15 until horses sufficiency from manage, harness etc was considered to Prepared to move detachment to 1st Indian Cavalry Divn area.	
6-2-15	Marched to ST. HILAIRE.	
7-2-15	ST. HILAIRE. One horse had carry from the lives during a storm at night. Of 6-2-15 and 7-2-15 and two manege established and two horses were left and no lie pressed and fin these horses Lent to Indian cavalry research. These two horses Lent to be exercised together with the lin manege horses — Clipping and tailing of horses. Refitting men and	Actual strength handed over to 1st Indian Cavalry Divn 38 rank and file 26 horses 20 vehicles -
ST. HILAIRE 8-2-15		

Army Form C. 2118.

WAR DIARY
or
INTELLIGENCE SUMMARY.
(Erase heading not required.)

Instructions regarding War Diaries and Intelligence Summaries are contained in F. S. Regs., Part II, and the Staff Manual respectively. Title pages will be prepared in manuscript.

Hour, Date, Place.	Summary of Events and Information.	Remarks and references to Appendices.
ST. HILAIRE 8-2-15 (cont) 9-2-15 to 16-2-15	Clearing barriers and equipment, clearing horses, making up teams and generally organising the whole detachment. As above. Weather generally very bad which greatly hindered work. Army route march.	
17-2-15	Weather bad. Medical examination of men paraded sick. Case of 11th of which 5 men sent to hospital. Attempted improvement in system of hooking over and shelter. Route march. Costs two hrs.	
18-2-15 19-2-15	Route march. Major Brennan arrived to meet C.R.E. 1st Army.	
20-2-15	Men awaiting equipment entries. Captain Clear reported arrival from leave. Major Brennan at Hd. Qrs. 1st Army. Recent orders to avail C.R.E. Ind. Div. 2nd horse work.	
21-2-15	Route march. Major Brennan returns orders for hunting with C.R.E. Indian Div. 2.	
22-2-15	Route march. Indian Cavalry Corps Ind. Div. settled scheme for different trenches. Major Brennan attended.	

Army Form C. 2118.

WAR DIARY
or
INTELLIGENCE SUMMARY.
(Erase heading not required.)

Instructions regarding War Diaries and Intelligence Summaries are contained in F. S. Regs., Part II, and the Staff Manual respectively. Title pages will be prepared in manuscript.

Hour, Date, Place.	Summary of Events and Information.	Remarks and references to Appendices.
23-2-15.	Route march.	
24-2-15.	Route march. Major Brenner visited site of trenches and surrounding fields	KM
25-2-15.	Seeing horses clipping, shoeing, harness inspection by officers. Major Brenner left Wilelaine and billeted in the area where trenches are being dug. Troops	KM KM
26-2-15.	Route march. Took over 8 heavy draught to light draught horses which arrived from the base.	KM
27-2-15.	Seeing, clipping &c	KM
28-2-15.	do.	KM

Drake
Major
1/3/15 for O.C. 1st Indian Field Squadron

WAR DIARY

1st Indian Field Squadron R.E. 1st Indian Cavalry Dn.

From 1st March 1915 To 31st March 1915

Confidential

War Diary
of
1st Indian Field Squadron S.E.
1st Indian Cavalry Division
O.E.F.

From 1st March 1915 to 31st March 1915

Army Form C. 2118.

Original

WAR DIARY
or
INTELLIGENCE SUMMARY.
(Erase heading not required.)

Instructions regarding War Diaries and Intelligence Summaries are contained in F. S. Regs., Part II, and the Staff Manual respectively. Title pages will be prepared in manuscript.

Hour, Date, Place.	Summary of Events and Information.	Remarks and references to Appendices.
March 1st	Major Brenner & Capt Wickham detached on duty building trenches in the vicinity of ST VENANT.	
2nd	The S & M Field troop engaged on their work. 3 forge wagons and 6 GS limbers temporarily transferred to Signal Squadron. Lieut Leslie and Major Evans went to ST VENANT to inspect work on trenches.	
3rd	Handed over 27 horses, 1 NCO & 13 men, 11 GS wagons to the CRA, 1st 9C Div. Lift Corporal injured from fall off horse and sent to hospital. 1 horse shot by orders of the Vet. officer, 1 horse died during night of colic.	
6th / 7th	2 Officers & 4 NCOs & 17 18th Lancers instructed in firing trench gun. Capt Leslie RE transferred to Meerut Div as CRE and departed in the morning. 2 officers & 6 Cavalry instructed in firing trench gun. The men, horses & its handed over to the CRA on 3/3/15 returned.	
9th / 10th	Major Evans went to ST OMER to see Chief Engineer GHQ. Horse shot by order of Veterinary officer. Division ordered to march Field Squadron to start fort.	
11th	Maj Brenner and Field troop marched. Maj Brenner and Field troop arrived in morning and proceeded with Capt Chase to AUCHEL in afternoon, with 2 horse & harness wagon from Field Squadron. Division marched in early morning.	

Army Form C. 2118.

WAR DIARY
or
INTELLIGENCE SUMMARY.
(Erase heading not required.)

Instructions regarding War Diaries and Intelligence Summaries are contained in F. S. Regs., Part II, and the Staff Manual respectively. Title pages will be prepared in manuscript.

Hour, Date, Place.	Summary of Events and Information.	Remarks and references to Appendices.
14/3/15.	Lt. H.G. Cresswell reported his arrival on being posted to the Indian Cavalry Division. Orders received at 6 p.m. for the squadron to move to LES PESSES arriving there by midnight. Squadron marched at 9 p.m. and arrived at LES PESSES at 10 p.m., where it was joined by the 2nd Deals Troop and Maj Brennan and Chase, they having marched from AUCHEL.	
15-3-15 LES PESSES	In billets ready to move at 2 hours notice. Picked out 14 horses done sick and injured.	Oct. 13
16.3.15.	In billets ready to move at 2 hours notice. Veterinary inspection — 5 horses for evacuated. Preparing loads —	Oct. 13
17.3.15.	In billets ready to move at 2 hours notice. 1 N.C.O. Horse Shoeing order of Veterinary Officers. Major EVANS left for England in connection with collection of information for 2nd Squadron.	AM/
18.3.15	A Bridges sent with one wagon & gr. of H.D. Horses to Legrand. Squadron for night. We have evacuated by order of Veterinary Officer.	AM/
Erny St Julien 19.3.15	Squadron moved 1600 dry to ERNY ST JULIEN.	AM/
20.3.15	Route march — Maj Brennan, Lt Cresswell, 2nd Troop & details for duty under 1st Army on Reconnoitre. Finishes at ST VENANT	AM/

Army Form C. 2118.

WAR DIARY
or
INTELLIGENCE SUMMARY.
(Erase heading not required.)

Instructions regarding War Diaries and Intelligence Summaries are contained in F. S. Regs., Part II, and the Staff Manual respectively. Title pages will be prepared in manuscript.

Hour, Date, Place.	Summary of Events and Information.	Remarks and references to Appendices.
SERNY 21-3-15.	The squadron marched today to SERNY. M de Grammont entertained us an hour from his day.	AM
22-3-15	Continued	AM
23-3-15	do	AM
24-3-15	do	AM.
25-3-15	In de Grammont interrupted upon his arrival today.	AM
26-3-15	Evening town.	AM
27-3-15	Rest march	AM
28-3-15.	"	AM
29-3-15.	"	AM
30-3-15	"	AM
31-3-15	"	AM/KaroljiMcZ

For officer commanding
1st Surrey Rein Squadron R.E.
1st 2nd Army Corps

Serial No. 48

12/5504

WAR DIARY

OF

1st Indian Field Squadron, R.E. 1st Indian Cavalry Div.

From 1st April 1915 to 30th April 1915

Army Form C. 2118.

WAR DIARY
or
INTELLIGENCE SUMMARY.

(Erase heading not required.)

Instructions regarding War Diaries and Intelligence Summaries are contained in F. S. Regs., Part II, and the Staff Manual respectively. Title pages will be prepared in manuscript.

Hour, Date, Place.	Summary of Events and Information.	Remarks and references to Appendices.
SERNY 1st to 5th April.	Exercising training horses &c.	H. Sloan Capt RE
SERNY 6th "	do — 6 Driver reinforcement arrived	H. Sloan Capt RE
" 7th "	do	H. Sloan Capt RE
" 8th "	do	H. Sloan Capt RE
" 9th – 16th "	horses do — 1 horse evacuated. —	H. Sloan Capt RE
" 17th "	do	H. Sloan Capt RE
" 18th – 19th "	do 1 horse evacuated	H. Sloan Capt RE
" 20th "	do	H. Sloan Capt RE
SERNY 21st "	do W. Wallach interpreter reported from sick leave	H. Sloan Capt RE
" 22nd "	do 1 heavy raining pants to { Division moved to MARIE CAPPLE hospital	H. Sloan Capt RE
" 26th – 30th incl	do — {9 heavy transport horses + 4 ordnance mules recd from remounts	H. Sloan Capt RE
		H. Sloan Capt RE

Serial No. 148

WAR DIARY
OF
1st Indian Field Squadron R.E.

From 1st May 1915 To 31st May 1915.

Army Form O. 2118.

Original

WAR DIARY
or
INTELLIGENCE SUMMARY.
(Erase heading not required.)

Instructions regarding War Diaries and Intelligence Summaries are contained in F.S. Regs., Part II, and the Staff Manual respectively. Title pages will be prepared in manuscript.

Hour, Date, Place.	Summary of Events and Information.	Remarks and references to Appendices.
SERNY –		
1.5.15 – 4.	Pen line	
4.5.15 –	do	
	Went into billets with Field Troops (2.SM.) night of 4/5.5.15. Squadron moved to LINGE and S.R.E.O and took	
5.5.15 – 6.	Grenvell.	
7.5.15 –	Pen line	
8.5.15 –	do	
9.5.15 –	do. One recruit from enrolled	
10.5.15 –	Arrived at WITTES.	
WITTES		
11.5.15 –	Rentine. Evacuated 2 horses 4 carts. Major Encrease R.E. and 67 O.R. R.E. joined from England	
12.5.15 –	In line line and poodery technical regim.	2 charger recd.
13.5.15 –	do	2 recruits hm enrolled
14.5.15 –	do	
15.5.15 –	Instruction on riding etc.	Capt. Clune left for England.
16.5.15 –	do	30 riding, horses and 4 work horses from R.D.
		Name of excellent quality – and in good condition. O.G.B.

Army Form C. 2118.

WAR DIARY
or
INTELLIGENCE SUMMARY.

(Erase heading not required.)

Instructions regarding War Diaries and Intelligence Summaries are contained in F.S. Regs., Part II, and the Staff Manual respectively. Title pages will be prepared in manuscript.

Hour, Date, Place.	Summary of Events and Information.	Remarks and references to Appendices.
WITTES 17-5-15-	Instruction in riding etc. Field Troop (S.S.M.) moved in with Div. Recing Gun at 2.30 p.m. 9 C.S. wagon returned to Orleans - 2 A.T. Carts with 4 mules sent to Divns. transferred on to A.S.C.	
18-5-15-	36 N.C.Os, Sappers & Drivers arrived from England. 5 mules & 2 limbered G.S. wagons received from Lieutenant Bryant and Sgt Drewler 17.1.C.D. Instructions in riding continued. Capt. Chase R.E. returned from England -	
19-5-15-	Instruction etc. 1 limbered G.S. wagon and 1 pair of horses received from Gen. Laidlaw Brigade 4 will Troop (S.S.M.) returned in evening - Instruction etc. 1 pair heavy draught horses and	
20-5-15-	1 G.S. wagon sent to Ballast ambulance -	
21-5-15-	2 limbers marched to Pelf. mule stables -	
22-5-15-		
23-5-15-	1 med. Officer & 2 O.R. R.A.M.C. reported arrival	

Army Form C. 2118.

WAR DIARY
or
INTELLIGENCE SUMMARY.

(Erase heading not required.)

Instructions regarding War Diaries and Intelligence Summaries are contained in F. S. Regs., Part II, and the Staff Manual respectively. Title pages will be prepared in manuscript.

Hour, Date, Place.	Summary of Events and Information.	Remarks and references to Appendices.
WITTES -		
24-5-15-	Routine -	
25-5-15-	Major Brenner appointed Field Squadron commander	
	Routine -	
26-5-15-	Routine -	
27-5-15-	marched to STAPLES -	
28-5-15-	marched to RUBROUCK -	
RUBROUCK		
29-5-15-	1 N.C.O. and 12 Sappers arrived from England. Field Troops (I.O.? M, moved up to front line. Capt. Clouse accompanied	
30-5-15-	2 men & two draft horses - Medical Officer sent up to Field	
31-5-15-	3 Indrail servants mounted - Troops (S.P.M.) Routine. Riding drill and troop training -	✗ Major Brenner's personal servants & ayah - Mr. Prattock's ayah -

A.G. Brenner
Major R.E.
Comdg 1st Indian Field Squadron

Serial No 148.

WAR DIARY
OF

1st Indian Field Squadron R.E.

From 1st June 1915 To 30th June 1915.

Army Form C. 2118.

WAR DIARY
or
INTELLIGENCE SUMMARY.
(Erase heading not required.)

Instructions regarding War Diaries and Intelligence Summaries are contained in F. S. Regs., Part II, and the Staff Manual respectively. Title pages will be prepared in manuscript.

Hour, Date, Place.	Summary of Events and Information.	Remarks and references to Appendices.
RUBRUCK. 1-6-15- 2-6-14- 3-6-14-	Routine. Lieut Warwick R.A.M.C. reported arrival from Field Troop. do do.	
4-6-15-	Received orders to move up to front line for work in vicinity of BRANDHOEK at 5.00 p.m. 3rd Divn. 2nd Army.	
NEAR BRANHOEK 5-6-15-	Squadron arrived in vicinity of BRANDHOEK at 5.00 p.m. Major Brennan met us on advance and sent on with Lt. Adjt. R.E. to an interview with Brennan he was informed that Field Squadron and Field Troop was transferred back to 1st & 2nd C.D. Divn. In formation received that Capt. Nickleson R.E. had been wounded on morning of 3.6.15- and evacuated. Verbal instructions received from G.S. 1st D. to bivouac & brush front ammunition. Majors Brennan & Evans visited HOOGE. Captn Glynne & Lt. Gresswell & Evans visited HOOGE.	
6-6-15-	Slightly command line approached and condition of locality. Enemy shelled main road at thorough YPRES about 6.00 p.m. 5.6.15- and again at 12.15 A.M. on 6.6.15- Continual Sapping work going on— SIALKOT and UMBALLA Brigades Relieved on new trench bombs. Squadron Officers & Troops Sergts reconnoitred approaches to HOOGE by night.	
7-6-15-	Routine — 6 horses received from "A" Bty. R.H.A.	

Army Form C. 2118.

WAR DIARY
or
INTELLIGENCE SUMMARY.
(Erase heading not required.)

Instructions regarding War Diaries and Intelligence Summaries are contained in F. S. Regs., Part II, and the Staff Manual respectively. Title pages will be prepared in manuscript.

Hour, Date, Place.	Summary of Events and Information.	Remarks and references to Appendices.
near BRANDHOEK. 8.6.15.	Routine. 4 horses received from G.O.C. "B" R.H.A. Completed indents for Officers 12 I.C.D. in lieu of Issued Grenades.	
9-6-15-	Routine. Training in bomb work was extensive work. Major Browne visited 12 Bridging train; to inspect light draught horses about to be transferred to 1st I.F. Squadron.	
10-6-15- 11-6-15-	Heavy thunder storm between 6.30 a.m. & 9.30 a.m. Received orders reporting to 3rd Div. H.Q. for work. 3rd Div. ordered work under G.O.C. 8th Brigade who instructed the O.C. F. Squadron to dig a trench over a bad piece in ground South of Rly. wood. Work been done on night of 10/11. 32 railway trucks sent to RUBROCK under orders of 14 Ind. Cavly. Div. — 1 officer and 80 other ranks detailed for work —	
12.6.15-	On night of 11-6-15 & 12-6-15. Squadron was ordered to connect up line of trenches held by Royal Scots in Railway wood with line held by Middlesex Regt. which ended in a hedge about 125 yds South of Royal Scots trench in Railway wood. This piece of ground was a low place 125 x 150 in front of German trenches and used to be swept by German machine gun fire. As there was the first time this new sector had been in added work, the	Map ZILLEBEKE 1/10 000

Army Form O. 2118.

WAR DIARY
or
INTELLIGENCE SUMMARY.
(Erase heading not required.)

Instructions regarding War Diaries and Intelligence Summaries are contained in F. S. Regs., Part II, and the Staff Manual respectively. Title pages will be prepared in manuscript.

Hour, Date, Place.	Summary of Events and Information.	Remarks and references to Appendices.
12-6-15-	front to be played over carefully rehearsed on night of 10-6-15-	
	11-6-15-. The men were very pleased and quietly gathered 1- and about 11.00 p.m. on 11-6-15- and in 40 nearwels had got out into the front with food even in front of their trenches. The holes were then joined up in the form of trenches dressed and made low across the places were small ramarks taught by 1100 a.m. on 12.6-15- where men were entirely. The Servicians were very at all colour and cheer. To be entirely hid themselves and they did appeared to be discovered about him from in tel about 12.45 a.m. on 12.6-15- when a party of the Middlesex were putting up props out wire entanglements in front of the new trench. They then received their surprise for a short time and being silent several were from the careful to take no further notice in the matter. Casualties our men wounded—	
13-6-15-	Went in close to entrench our night of 12-6-15- and	

13-6-15

WAR DIARY or INTELLIGENCE SUMMARY.

Army Form C. 2118.

(Erase heading not required.)

Instructions regarding War Diaries and Intelligence Summaries are contained in F. S. Regs., Part II, and the Staff Manual respectively. Title pages will be prepared in manuscript.

Hour, Date, Place.	Summary of Events and Information.	Remarks and references to Appendices.
YPRES – 13-6-15-	In evening orders 3 Officers took over & handed & reconnoitre" the nights work and men were marching. Tel: it has clearly enough for them before in the order for work men cancelled and a telephone message was sent & handed to await this Officers. Orders were afterwards received to move back over Zerry at 5.00 am on 14-6-15-	
14-6-15-	Marched to LE BRIARDE and went into billets for night.	
15-6-15- BLAMART 16-6-15	Proceeded to BLAMART and went into bivouac.	
17-6-15-	O.C. visited ST. MARTIN to arrange exchange of livery for light draught horses with O.C. 1st Pontoon Train. Squadron and Field Troop were informally inspected by G.O.C. 1. C. Corps. Field Squadron was complimented on work at YPRES. Received 34 ricketry and 4 L.D. Casements. Also 9 cast horses from "C" R.H.A. 22 L.D. horses belong to 17.	
18-6-15-	Relieved 28 H.D. on Bridging Train R.E.	
19-6-15-	Two horses missing from A.V.H.A. Our horses from bivouac on account of broken leg. Evacuated 1 horse and 2 mules on account of injuries.	

Army Form C. 2118.

WAR DIARY
or
INTELLIGENCE SUMMARY.
(Erase heading not required.)

Instructions regarding War Diaries and Intelligence Summaries are contained in F. S. Regs., Part II, and the Staff Manual respectively. Title pages will be prepared in manuscript.

Hour, Date, Place.	Summary of Events and Information.	Remarks and references to Appendices.
BLARMART.		
20-6-15-		
21-6-15-	Run Lui Recet Post Nieun reported occupied at ab 2.0 $\frac{6}{15}$	
22-6-15-	1 N.C.O. 5 Sappers 3 Drivers 6 horses & 1 waggon now ordered to Cups 1st Bat Div - R.M.	
23-6-15-	Aire detachment relieved and 10 Sappers from S.B.M. now employed Makersheyd in their place. Have received list account injury. Run lui	
24-6-15-		
25-6-15-		
26-6-15-	Sappers reported for work at Cups Nord Div on 23 $\frac{6}{15}$. Run lui	
27-6-15-		
28-6-15-	O.C. reported to C.E. 1st Army. Received orders for work at front. Reported to C.E. Indian Corps in evening and arranged programme for tomorrow entering frontier. Orders sent out for 12 N.C.D & had disposal of Indians.	
29-6-15-	Cups for work and no recce in evening Leadperlan	
30-6-15-	Recce on work in Pres du Pond. I think indictes N.B. freuch $\frac{1}{4}$ Z5& B3 E5 and 1 with 4 ESTAIRES. de mairs from. Work dor6 at 8.00 am in	

Army Form C. 2118.

WAR DIARY
or
INTELLIGENCE SUMMARY.

(Erase heading not required.)

Instructions regarding War Diaries and Intelligence Summaries are contained in F. S. Regs., Part II, and the Staff Manual respectively. Title pages will be prepared in manuscript.

Hour, Date, Place.	Summary of Events and Information.	Remarks and references to Appendices.
FONE. 30.6.15 (cont)	out out outposts front —	A.W. Browning Major C.S. Commanding 1st Indian Field general Hd.

Serial No. 148.

121/6502

WAR DIARY
OF
1st Indian Field Squadron.

FROM 1st July 1915 TO 31st July 1915

Army Form C. 2118.

WAR DIARY
or
INTELLIGENCE SUMMARY.
(Erase heading not required.)

Instructions regarding War Diaries and Intelligence Summaries are contained in F. S. Regs., Part II, and the Staff Manual respectively. Title pages will be prepared in manuscript.

Hour, Date, Place.	Summary of Events and Information.	Remarks and references to Appendices.
FOSSE 1-7-15	The Squadron was distributed on 30.6.15 as follows "A" Troop at FOSSE for working under C.R.E. LAHORE Divn. "B" " " " " " " " with billeting Sec. and Headquarters "C" " " ZELOBES for work under C.R.E. MEERUT Divn. "D" " " ESTAIRES " " " " 51st Divn.	Capt. Chase in ETON post. Major Evans R.E. Lieut. Gaskell on FOSSE Bridge Road. Lieut. Reft. Kerr on Muddy Lane and 2 Drury post. Meerut Divn. & "C" Troop working on 3 posts E6.
2-7-15	As on 1/15.	
3-7-15	As on 2/15.	
4-7-15	O.C. visited all C.R.E's of Divn. & C.E. Indian Corps and all ends. Brought 5 lorry loads from LILLERS. Accompany for supplies came through C.R.E's of Divn. 2½ limits. On Batry. Lnt. R.E. (Temp) reported arrival.	
5-7-15	"C" Troop working on A.6. post from 4/15. Enemy shelling vicinity all interval but no shells have fallen on the Batn.	
6-7-15	Remained engaged as before.	
7-7-15	Working parties as before. do.	

Army Form C. 2118.

WAR DIARY
or
INTELLIGENCE SUMMARY.
(Erase heading not required.)

Instructions regarding War Diaries and Intelligence Summaries are contained in F. S. Regs., Part II, and the Staff Manual respectively. Title pages will be prepared in manuscript.

Hour, Date, Place.	Summary of Events and Information.	Remarks and references to Appendices.
FOSSE. 8-7-15-	29th Cavalry working on communication trench from EUSTON Post to	
9-7-15-	PONT LOGY. Remainder as before except party in 57th Div. digging unit in LA GORGUE bridgehead. 29th Lancers returned trench on ETON and CHELTENHAM posts. Remainder as before.	
10-7-15-	LAHORE DIV. party started work on CLIFTON N. post. 29th Lancers started a communication trench close to NEUVE CHAPPELLE. Remainder as before. (night work)	
11-7-15-	Squadron 29th Lancers withdrawn from work. Remainder as before.	
12-7-15-	As on 10-7-15-. 19th 1 Squadron of 9th Lancers working on communication trench near NEUVE CHAPPELLE at night. Remainder as before.	
13-7-15-	6th Lancers withdrawn from the E. Cav. posts and put on FOSSE bridge Guard. Remainder as before except 19th Lancers all working on ETON and CHELTEN-HAM posts.	
14-7-15-	As on 13/7/15-. Major in Evans R.E. reported departures for trench employment in 51st Div.	

WAR DIARY
or
INTELLIGENCE SUMMARY.
(Erase heading not required.)

Army Form C. 2118.

Instructions regarding War Diaries and Intelligence Summaries are contained in F. S. Regs., Part II, and the Staff Manual respectively. Title pages will be prepared in manuscript.

Hour, Date, Place.	Summary of Events and Information.	Remarks and references to Appendices.
FOSSE		
15-7-15-	As on 14/7/15	
16-7-15-	" " 15/7/15	
17-7-15-	Working parties relieved. Relief of Bde completed on 19/7/15 when New but he 3 Section of men (Brigade) of 400 men each, 1st D.G. turnoff at night in cases heard N.E. of NEUVE CHAPPELLE.	
18-7-15-	1st D.G. finished night work with no casualties. 2nd Lancers started work on one of Lnt Newton's projects. Remainder as before.	
19-7-15-	As on 18.7.15. Lucknow Divn started work on line at ROUGE CROIX.	
20-7-15-	As on 19.7.15. Brigade	
21-7-15-	As on 20-7-15. Scullett Searly renewed work on La Gorgue. Bridge Head and started working on Le Drumez.	
22-7-15-	Lucknow Brigade decided work on KEARY post - Remainder as before.	51st
23 & 24-7-15-	As on 22-7-15.	
25-7-15-	As on 22-7-15. Handed over all works in Meerut and Lahore Divn. areas to Major Turner R.E. Lahore Divn.	

Army Form C. 2118.

WAR DIARY
or
INTELLIGENCE SUMMARY.
(Erase heading not required.)

Instructions regarding War Diaries and Intelligence Summaries are contained in F. S. Regs., Part II, and the Staff Manual respectively. Title pages will be prepared in manuscript.

Hour, Date, Place.	Summary of Events and Information.	Remarks and references to Appendices.
26-7-15- (FOSSE)	As on 25-7-15. Received orders to return to Div¹ Hd. Qrs. on 29.7.15. but at night these orders were superseded by others which allowed date of march to 28-7-15- All men recalled from work & furnished 1st Div⁻	
27-7-15-	Collected tools & material. Handed over tools to C.R.E. Meerut and certain tools borrowed from Tulloches Brigade. Packed supplies etc. for march on 28-7-15. Handed over horses in 51st & false Div⁻ areas & Major Ferrer R.E and those in Meerut Div⁻ area to C.R.E. Meerut, Sent note on route to be completed to Chief Engineer, Indian Corps.	
28-7-15-	Marched to Regterie West.	
29-7-15- to 31-7-15-	Halted at Regterie West.	

A.G. Brenner
Major R.E.
Comdg. 1st Indian Field Squadron
R.E.
1st Indian Cavalry Div⁻

Serial No. 148

121/6948

WAR DIARY
OF

1st Indian Field Squadron, R.E., 1st Indian Cavalry Division.

FROM 1st August 1915 To 31st August 1915.

Army Form C. 2118

WAR DIARY

or

INTELLIGENCE SUMMARY.

(Erase heading not required.)

Instructions regarding War Diaries and Intelligence Summaries are contained in F. S. Regs., Part II, and the Staff Manual respectively. Title pages will be prepared in manuscript.

Hour, Date, Place.	Summary of Events and Information.	Remarks and references to Appendices.
Regutaine W		
1-8-15-	Marched to HEZECQUES area	[initials]
2-8-15-	" " AUBIN ST. VAST-	[initials]
3-8-15-	" " MESNIL DOMQUEUR,	[initials]
4-8-15-	" " DOMART-	[initials]
5-8-15-	Half at DOMART overhauling drets-	[initials]
6-8-15-	" refitting & training-	[initials]
7-8-15-	" "	[initials]
8-10/8/15	" "	[initials]
11/8/15	Ditto. Major Brunner instructed officers of the Sialkot Brigade in bomb throwing; types of bombs used Nos 1, 2, 5, 6, 8 & "Pitcher". There was a slight accident with a No 5 bomb and Maj. Brunner was struck by a fragment in the shoulder. He was admitted to hospital and the command of the squadron devolved on Maj W H Evans RE.	[initials]
12/8/15.	Training continued. Maj Evans instructed the Lucknow Brigade in bomb throwing. No 5 bomb was not used by order of the Div.	[initials]
13/8/15.	Training continued. Maj Brunn instructed the Ambala Brigade in bomb throwing.	[initials]
14/8/15.	30 chemical bombs containing sulphur dioxide, tried in the presence of the Gas expert 3rd Army and the SAS MS of the Division.	[initials]

WAR DIARY
or
INTELLIGENCE SUMMARY.
(Erase heading not required.)

Army Form C. 2118

Instructions regarding War Diaries and Intelligence Summaries are contained in F. S. Regs., Part II, and the Staff Manual respectively. Title pages will be prepared in manuscript.

Hour, Date, Place.	Summary of Events and Information.	Remarks and references to Appendices.
15/8/15.	Maj Evans visited the trenches held by the 2nd Division, with a view to ascertaining the nature of the RE work to be done. 15 horses were Dismounted by order of the SAS R and 7 horses were received from the Corps Remount section.	
16/8/15.	Maj Evans visited Chief Engineer, 3rd Army at BEAUQUESNE, RE Park at ACHEUX and returned No 5 Mills powder to Ammunition Railhead.	
19/8/15.	Maj Evans & Capt Charre visited trenches held by 2 and 3 C. Div and examined work being done by the 2nd 3rd F. Squadron.	
21/8/15.	Capt Charre, Lieut Cresswell, 4 sergeants, 30 other ranks, 4 horses and vedettes were proceeded to MARTINSART as an advanced party, to take over work from 2nd F. Squadron.	
22/8/15.	The squadron less cart carts, two waggons, horns and 7 sappers from troop marched to the road E. of FORCEVILLE and bivouacked on right. Remainder remained at SOMART under Lt Gammon. Advanced portion of squadron marched in to MARTINSART and took over RE work in secto AUTHUILLE – HAMEL of front line from 2nd Indian Field Squadron.	
27/8/15.	Took over defences of sector Eg hill (eg) in Indian Cavalry Division and in defences of the village of AUTHUILLE. Looking position obtained from Lochnagar Brigade in reserve in AUTHUILLE and form firing line.	

Army Form C. 2118

WAR DIARY
or
INTELLIGENCE SUMMARY.
(Erase heading not required.)

Instructions regarding War Diaries and Intelligence Summaries are contained in F. S. Regs., Part II, and the Staff Manual respectively. Title pages will be prepared in manuscript.

Hour, Date, Place.	Summary of Events and Information.	Remarks and references to Appendices.
25 – 8 – 14.	Work on defences continued; B troop sent to work in sub-sector G.1; C troop sub-sector G.2; A & B troops AUTHUILLE defences and approaches from MARTINSART.	
26 – 8 – 14.	Work on defences continued. Our division inspected us.	
27 – 8 – 14.	Work and " " " " "	
28 – 8 – 14.	" " " " "	
29 – 8 – 14.	" " " " "	
30 – 8 – 14.	" " " " 2 horses wounded in neck.	
31 – 8 – 14.	" "	

[signature]
Major R.E.
O.C. 1st Field Squadron R.E.
1/9/15.

Serial No. 148.

Confidential

121/7286

War Diary

of

1st Indian Field Squadron R.E.

FROM 1st September 1915. TO 30th September 1915.

Army Form C. 2118

WAR DIARY
or
INTELLIGENCE SUMMARY.
(Erase heading not required.)

Instructions regarding War Diaries and Intelligence Summaries are contained in F. S. Regs., Part II, and the Staff Manual respectively. Title pages will be prepared in manuscript.

Hour, Date, Place.	Summary of Events and Information.	Remarks and references to Appendices.
September 1st	Advanced portion of squadron employed on defensive works, G section, (AUTHUILLE–OVILLIERS road to HAMEL) and in defences AUTHUILLE village. Handing over to 2nd Indian Div. squadron commenced.	
2nd	Advanced portion of squadron marched to BEAUCOURT. Handed over from line to 2nd Indian Div. squadron, one officer, one N.C.O. & many others.	
3rd/4th	Halt at BEAUCOURT awaiting orders. Lt Craswell went on 7 days leave.	
5th	Capt Chance and B Troop ordered up to SENLIS to supervise digging. 1st & 2nd war details attached. Advanced portion of squadron less B Troop marched to DOMART to furnish billets, rejoining party left behind. 15 horses received as remounts.	
6th	Squadron marched to ETOILE on SOMME in remounting, returning in evening and commenced training in Sunbray meet equipment.	
7th	Training in riding continued.	
8th	"	
9th	"	
10th	Day spent in cleaning up and arranging for train in trenches. Squadron & horses all were left to look after in charge of. Lt Rositer left to MARTINSART to commence taking over work. Evacuated 10 horses and all 10 from remounts.	
11th	BEAUCOURT. Lt Craswell returned from leave to DOMART.	

Army Form C. 2118

WAR DIARY
or
INTELLIGENCE SUMMARY.

(Erase heading not required.)

Instructions regarding War Diaries and Intelligence Summaries are contained in F. S. Regs., Part II, and the Staff Manual respectively. Title pages will be prepared in manuscript.

Hour, Date, Place.	Summary of Events and Information.	Remarks and references to Appendices.
September 12th	Advanced portion of squadron marched to MARTINSART. G section RE. were taken over from 2nd & 3rd Squadrons. Capt Chave put in charge of all work in first line & supports, Lt Gresswell of all work in 2nd line, Lt Taylor over line AUTHVILLE, 1st 2nd to HAMEL in evening. Infantim received orders to return to billets in evening.	[signature]
13th	At HAMEL squadron developed Clusters of ROUGLONE; all horses at SAENGOTSL, Capt Chave & R troops rejoined from SENLIS.	[signature]
14th	Squadron employed party cavalry day & night on work, horses on SOMME watered for Clusters by section Coy.	[signature]
15th	DOMART work continued on before.	[signature]
16th	Work continued as before. Lt Gausson arrived & Sec 51st Div. signal section with three despatch riders under Capt Chave, also received to hand over line AUTHVILLE to 2/3 work continued in moving & strengthening defences which Advanced portion of squadron left billets in evening Highland Field Coy. Capt Chave on his return in afternoon. 1v 2v Coy for relieved by Highland S.Co.	[signature]
17th	Advanced portion of squadron returned to permanent billets at DOMART. Capt Chave rejoined. 2 horses shot for Glanders and 9 others suspected inspected.	[signature]
18th	Instruction in bridging & troop drill continued. Remaining horses wallowed.	[signature]

Army Form C. 2118.

WAR DIARY
or
INTELLIGENCE SUMMARY.
(Erase heading not required.)

Instructions regarding War Diaries and Intelligence Summaries are contained in F. S. Regs., Part II, and the Staff Manual respectively. Title pages will be prepared in manuscript.

Hour, Date, Place.	Summary of Events and Information.	Remarks and references to Appendices.
September 19th	Training in kindjying and temp drill continued. Capt chase went on 7 days leave.	
" 20th	Preparation made for troops parading with pack transport, mts, tools in park saddles & in tool buckets. Major Evans attended a divisional Staff ride.	
" 21st	Division paraded near DOMART for inspection by Lord Kitchener.	
" 22nd	Division moved to new billeting area. Squadron marched at 12.50 p.m. to OUTREBOIS, arriving 3.50 p.m. Horse suspected as glandered is — and new remounts received. Squadron declared free from glanders.	
" 23rd	Training continued.	
" 24th	Do	
" 25th	Do	
" 26th	Do Squadron placed at 2 hours notice.	
" 27th	Do 2 days in rations drawn. Squadron placed at 2 hours notice. Major Mennier rejoined.	
" 28th	Do Squadron put again on 2½ hours notice.	
" 29th	Do Major Bradbury left to join 23rd div as CRE.	
" 30th	Do	

Swang
Major RD
OC 1st IV 3rd Dn Squadron.

Serial No. 148.

Confidential

121/7601

War Diary

of

1st Indian Field Squadron R.E.

FROM 1st October 1915. TO 31st October 1915.

Army Form C. 2118.

CE/2/5
22/11/15

WAR DIARY
INTELLIGENCE SUMMARY.
(Erase heading not required.)

Instructions regarding War Diaries and Intelligence Summaries are contained in F. S. Regs., Part II, and the Staff Manual respectively. Title pages will be prepared in manuscript.

Hour, Date, Place.	Summary of Events and Information.	Remarks and references to Appendices.
Oct 1st 1915.	Divisional field day. Field Squadron employed on building two floating bridges across the River AUTHIE at MEZEROLLES and OUTREBOIS: bridges erected in ¾ hour & 1½ hours respectively; spans about 40'. Serious defect in equipment discovered; never section with male ends only unlashed, it was supported only on that side. All lower sections should have female ends and shores made by Sapper.	W.H.
2nd 1915.	Training in bridging at MEZEROLLES	CW
3rd 1915.	Near MEZEROLLES: bridge 108' long constructed in 1 hour and upstream of 6th Cavalry found over into 16 bd hours to a minute.	CW
4th 1915.	2 troops bridging near OCCOCHES; 2 troops practising demolition of railway bridges at H.E.M. Squadron of 17th Lancers worked	CW
5th 1915.	Divisional field day. Squadron employed in preparing 3 bridges over River AUTHIE for demolition.	CW
6th 1915.	Training in demolition of bridges	CW
7th "	Training in bridging (2 troops), demolition (2 troops)	CW
8th "	Divisional field day. Squadron employed in building a bridge at OUTREBOIS.	CW
9th "	Training in troop drill (2 troops), bridging (2 troops)	CW
10th "	Horses received and men given a half holiday	CW

WAR DIARY
INTELLIGENCE SUMMARY.
(Erase heading not required.)

Army Form C. 2118.

Instructions regarding War Diaries and Intelligence Summaries are contained in F.S. Regs., Part II, and the Staff Manual respectively. Title pages will be prepared in manuscript.

Hour, Date, Place.	Summary of Events and Information.	Remarks and references to Appendices.
October 11th 1915	One troop practising demolition of railway line; 3 troops digging approaches for bridge.	
12 "	Squadron employed in building 3 bridges near OUTREBOIS: 2 single bridge and one double bridge constructed. Single bridge commenced pouring over bridge at 11 am; cavalry brigade commenced pouring over bridge at 11 am; cavalry all over by 12 noon. Q battery (18 vehicles) over by 12.15 pm and A echelon of brigade over by 12.30 pm. One broad bridge was broken & replaced in 20 minutes. We have had occasion to broach. Troop 10 minutes to broach. Decided that the double bridge offered few advantages; nature mud in the single file; most in canvas screen in water led in single file; most in canvas screen in the sides were dangerous, in that they cross horses a feature soured of security.	
13 "	Squadron marched to DOMART into billets previously occupied.	
14 "	Squadron employed on cleaning and making boats. O.C. went on leave in am. Squadron in stopt idem.	
15 "	Divisional field day. Squadron marched 10 miles to LE MEILLARD thru 5 to BERNAVILLE where a troop was attached to the 2 leading brigades, which advanced to FIEFFES and dug themselves in troop country; one troop with demolition parties from regiments sent on a special mission to destroy railway junction and bridges at CANAPLES. One troop in support of rear Bde during advance guard action into communication with troops with brigades.	

Army Form C. 2118.

WAR DIARY
or
INTELLIGENCE SUMMARY.

(Erase heading not required.)

Instructions regarding War Diaries and Intelligence Summaries are contained in F. S. Regs., Part II, and the Staff Manual respectively. Title pages will be prepared in manuscript.

Hour, Date, Place.	Summary of Events and Information.	Remarks and references to Appendices.
Bonnart 16th	Training in troops drill	
" 17th	Exercise and half holiday for men	
" 18th	Squadron employed on building at ETOILE, it was out on divisional manoeuvres.	
" 19th	Training in reconnaissance and skill activities. Major WH Snow purchased on 3 days leave	
Bonnart 20th	Squadron drill and Sapper training in the afternoon	
Domart 21st	"	
LIOMER 22nd	Squadron marched to LIOMER.	
" 23rd	Troop training	
" 24th	" "	
" 25th	" "	
" 26th	" " Maj WH Snow returned from leave. Le Rouskan Pierredes on leave.	
" 27th	Troop training.	
" 28th	Squadron drill.	
" 29th	Troop drill. Half the horses watered, owing to a burn caused by mill having flooded stables at ABBEVILLE,	
" 30th	Troop drill. Remaining horses watered	
" 31st	Exercise and half holiday for men	

Signature
W. H. [Snow]
Major pro
O.C. N 2nd 2d Squadron

Serial No. 148

121/7780

Confidential

War Diary

of

1st Indian Field Squadron R.E.

FROM 1st November 1915 TO 30th November 1915

WAR DIARY / INTELLIGENCE SUMMARY

Army Form C. 2118.

CR/501
9 DEC 1915

Hour, Date, Place.	Summary of Events and Information.	Remarks and references to Appendices.
L10 MER. Nov 1st 1915.	Horses inspected by G.O.C Division. Maj Evans and Capt Chase inspected transport duty by C.T.H.	
2nd	Very wet day.	
3rd	Two hours of S troop drill; found to have chandron. Reservists declared free. All horses blanketed to free through disinfector. All horses of S Troop soaked in creosote bath. A.R.S instructor late inauguration. 5th Gunners went on leave	
4th	Training continued. Maj Evans accompanied G.O.C Div to visit G.O.C 51 W Div at SENLIS with view to the employment of R.E. in Div. Also visited 3rd Cav Corps Head Qrs (late Canadas) to arrange if Squadrons of either div should co-operate in manoeuvres not yet known. Res Rev returned from leave.	
5th	Maj Evans & Capt Chase went up to MARTINSART (with inspectors) work done on G Sector work & view to Gathering event. Found there was a lot of R.E. work, so content to give S.O.S and prepared that both Squadrons (1st & 2nd S.O.S) should remain up permanently and commence to relieve 25% weekly.	
6th	Training continued. Maj Evans saw OC 2nd St Squadron and G.O.C 2nd Div with object of proposed to use both Squadrons in trenches. Reported accordingly to G.H.Q. in 90 Div.	
7th	Men given a half holiday, weekly only.	
8th	Gen Joffre of Div for presentation of French decorations by G.O.C IX Corps between TAILLY and LE QUESNOY. No 3866 Artif. Troop Sergeant Major E. Bamberger, R.H. (2nd D.O.S.M) awarded the Medaille Militaire for Gallant conduct. No 1777 Sapper S McCaul awarded the Croix de Guerre, having been mentioned in dispatches when employed with the Signal Coy, 22nd Brigade.	

Army Form C. 2118.

WAR DIARY
INTELLIGENCE SUMMARY.
(Erase heading not required.)

Instructions regarding War Diaries and Intelligence Summaries are contained in F. S. Regs., Part II, and the Staff Manual respectively. Title pages will be prepared in manuscript.

Hour, Date, Place.	Summary of Events and Information.	Remarks and references to Appendices.
LIOMER, Nov 9 1915	Capt Chase instructed the Lieutenant Private in the use of the ball hand Grenade. Maj Evans went to DC Corps HQ to discuss the employment of RE in the months of adjustments (not being trained from the Corps (7 2 brigades). Decided to have a CRE & 2 Squadrons each of 3 Troops, 1 Troops for squadrons being withdrawn tactics to look after horses. Strongly urged the desirability of getting rid of all sharp horses during the winter thereby reducing 2 squadrons each of 4 Troops.	
10 "	Troops drill. Very wet day.	
11 "	Squadron paraded with Indian Cavalry Corps for inspection by GOC 3rd Army at LE QUESNOY.	
12 "	Troop training.	
13 "	Hurricane in morning. Troops country	
14 "	Men given a half holiday. Divisional orders	
15 "	Capt Cresswell employed on attaching 38th to C94 in trench warfare.	
16 "	Copt Cresswell continued instruction of C94. No 1 Evans went a lecture to 2 & 3 Lewis on trench warfare	
17 "	by Capt Kerr employed in teaching 6th Dragoons trench warfare	
18 "	Capt Chase employed on teaching C94 trench warfare	
19 "	Major Evans accompanied Gen Sir during inspection at C94 in trench warfare. Maj Evans presented TSM Bantry at with the medaille militaire on a general parade	
20 "	Maj Evans discussed with SW staff the establishment of a timed workforce behind at LIOMER	

Army Form C. 2118.

WAR DIARY
or
INTELLIGENCE SUMMARY.
(Erase heading not required.)

Instructions regarding War Diaries and Intelligence Summaries are contained in F. S. Regs., Part II, and the Staff Manual respectively. Title pages will be prepared in manuscript.

Hour, Date, Place.	Summary of Events and Information.	Remarks and references to Appendices.
LIOMER. Nov 21st 1915	Men given a half holiday. Syllabus and time table prepared for Trench warfare school.	
" 22nd "	Troops employed in issuing tools and collecting (surcharge)	
" 23rd "	Squadron paraded at BOISRAULT at 11.30 am for inspection by GOC as a dismounted field squadron of 3 troops for work with a dismounted division formed from the 3rd Cav. Divn. Capt. Clare appointed as OC of the squadron for dismounted work under this division is called out and major transp as OC of the division is Troops employed on digging trenches and construction troughs.	
" 24th "		
" 25 "	Major Evans visited R& Park, RIBEMONT, to arrange for tools and stores for Trench warfare school. Troops employed on fieldworks	
" 26 "	Troops employed on fieldworks	
" 27 "	Major Evans with shovels, batman and clerk handed at 11 am at WIRY with dismounted division staff as CRE of the division. Troops employed in fieldworks.	
" 28 "	Half holiday for men - only parades for horses. 12 British, 6 Indian officers, 12 British and 2 Indian NCOs arrived as students for the Trench warfare class.	
" 29 "	Class commenced at 9 am with lectures on Scope of work and General principles of Trench work. NCOs employed in establishing huts etc, GOC visited class. Lectures in afternoon on tools and materials.	
" 30 "	A troop with 2Lt Gammon sent in detachment to Lucheux Bridge at ZONG PRE to build shelter. 21 men of 17th K.G.O. knights lancers arrived and remained to look after their horses. Class given lectures on details of trenches in morning and outside in afternoon.	

Signed
Major RE
OC 1st KG Indian Field Squadron RE
30/11/15

War Diary
of
1st. Indian Field Sqn. RE

November. 1915.

SERIAL NO. 148.

Confidential

War Diary

of

1st Indian Field Squadron, R.E.

FROM 1st December 1915. **TO** 31st December 1915.

Army Form C. 2118.

WAR DIARY
of
INTELLIGENCE SUMMARY.
(Erase heading not required.)

Instructions regarding War Diaries and Intelligence Summaries are contained in F. S. Regs., Part II, and the Staff Manual respectively. Title pages will be prepared in manuscript.

Hour, Date, Place.	Summary of Events and Information.	Remarks and references to Appendices.
LIOMER. 1st December/15	Trench warfare class. Lecture by Capt Edwards, 1/Beds Regt. RE intelligence lecture on obstacles in the offensive. NCOs on practical work	
2nd "	Lecture on revetment and drainage. " "	
3rd "	" " " working parties, blocking trenches " "	
4th "	" " " RE implements and shelters " "	
5th "		
6th "	Modeling for Trench warfare School. Troop horses put to grass —	
7th "	Defence of villages and defence of woods —	
8th "	Lecture first Demolition	
9th "	Commanding Offr Emergency Tgraph "LIOMER Station" and Bridges - Troop training - carrying out dummy trenches near town step.	
10th "	Route march for the squadron.	
11th "	Troop Train — filling up trenches dug for Trench warfare School	
12th "	Troop Train — filling up trenches dug for Trench warfare School	
13th "	do.	
14th "	do.	
15th "	Maj Evans returned from leave. Capt Chown proceeded on leave. Squadron ordered to move billets. 20 Sappers, 12 drivers joined as dismounted reinforcements and	

Army Form C. 2118.

WAR DIARY
or
INTELLIGENCE SUMMARY.
(Erase heading not required.)

Instructions regarding War Diaries and Intelligence Summaries are contained in F. S. Regs., Part II, and the Staff Manual respectively. Title pages will be prepared in manuscript.

Hour, Date, Place.	Summary of Events and Information.	Remarks and references to Appendices.
EMBREVILLE Dec 16th 1915	"D" Squadron marched to EMBREVILLE (20 miles) Day spent cutting into billets, a matter of some difficulty	
" 17 "	Troop training	
" 18 "	Men given half holiday. Horses exercised in morning	
" 19 "	Sappers employed on digging entrenchments & cutting brushwood for the French trench system school. Grooms employed on cutting brushwood and cleaning the stables	
" 20 "	Do.	
" 21 "	Do. Maj Evans attended some conference regarding a trench attack scheme.	
" 22 "	2Lt Gammon investigated question of underground shelters for the underground brigade and found that constructing accommodation could be used. Construction of a hut giving accommodation at GAMACHES for Corps wireless commenced.	
" 23 "	Sappers employed on field works for French trench system school	
" 24 "	Do.	
" 25 "	Xmas day. Men given a holiday. Capt Chase returned from leave.	
" 26 "	Sunday. Men given half holiday. Horses exercised.	
" 27 "	Sappers employed on Falsworks. Maj Evans, Capt. Chanty, and Capt Kerr visited camouflage school in AMIENS and French mortar school at VALMEUREUX.	
" 28 "	Sappers employed on fieldworks. Maj Evans attended conference on a trench attack scheme. Statements for 2 French Confrere classes wanted. Lt Jorgenson went on leave.	
" 29 "	Lecture by Maj Evans on General principles by Capt Chase on details of trenches. Capt. Carroll in took a material. Leigham and Caen revetting. Lt Gammon again investigated question of shelters for LUCKNOW Brigade	

Army Form C. 2118

WAR DIARY
or
INTELLIGENCE SUMMARY.
(Erase heading not required.)

Instructions regarding War Diaries and Intelligence Summaries are contained in F. S. Regs., Part II, and the Staff Manual respectively. Title pages will be prepared in manuscript.

Hour, Date, Place.	Summary of Events and Information.	Remarks and references to Appendices.
EMBREVILLE. Dec 30th 1915	Capt Chave reported his departure on transfer to the 79th Dn Coy RE, 18th Divn at ALBERT. French supper class Capt General acted on reinforcements. Maj Evans in command. Capt Raiz Ram on photographs. Capt Carnwell gave lecture to Subadar, Maj Evans inspected was between SARGNIES and BEAU-CHAMPS, which required repairs urgently. Arrangements made with the Sapper posts & chauffeurs for supply of metal & a roller.	
31"	Horses were machined on 29th and today finally passed as fit from Glanders. French reinforcements laying were today lectured on shelter, loopholes &c. and were today lectured in machine gun emplacements. Capt Carnwell gave lecture on defences of works, Indian reinforcement employed on Rail Ram in defences & watches. General lecture on something.	

L.I. Evans
Major RE
OC, W Indian Field Squadron RE

1/1/16

War Diary
First Indian
Field Sqn RE
First Indian Cav
Div
Dec: 1915

SERIAL NO. 146.

Confidential

War Diary

of

1st Indian Field Squadron R.E.

FROM 1st January 1918 TO 31st January 1918

Army Form C. 2118.

WAR DIARY
INTELLIGENCE SUMMARY.
(Erase heading not required.)

Instructions regarding War Diaries and Intelligence Summaries are contained in F. S. Regs., Part II, and the Staff Manual respectively. Title pages will be prepared in manuscript.

Hour, Date, Place.		Summary of Events and Information	Remarks and references to Appendices.
EMBREVILLE Jan 1st 1916		Holiday for Trench Warfare School. Troops training. Hut for winders at GAMACHES completed. Repair of road DARGNIES — GAMACHES begun. Lt Gammon proceeded on leave.	
"	2nd "	Lt Rich Ken returned to Trench Warfare School on Exploring and demolitions in morning: statistics in afternoon. Capt Crossman lectured to Sidings in boards. Work on road continued.	
"	3rd "	4 HQe wagons employed in carting metal, 20 labours in breaking metal, 70 RQe in laying metal. Capt Gammell lectured to Trench Warfare School on tunnels and the trench boat run. Maj Bowen on attacks & counter attacks. Capt Simpson RHA on artillery co-operation. Class ended. Work on road continued.	
"	4th "	Troops employed in digging trenches. Road work continued.	
"	5th "	Rerun (& lony) of 21st from French authorities at MARTAINE-VILLE. Road work continued. Runts went to Squadron in morning. Capt Cromwell went on leave.	
"	6th "	Road work continued and training to Canadians continued. Maj Dewey inspected horses in 5th area in car.	
"	7th "	Road work & Canadian training continued. Maj Evans continued inspection in car. Lt Jorgensen returned from leave.	
"	8th "	Parade in Squadrons for marching order. Road work & Canadian training continued.	
"	9th "	Troops own half holiday. Road work continued. Cpls VA Debril with 2 batmen & 2 drivers reported his arrival from 2A cav Regt in transfer. Lt Gammon returned from leave.	

Army Form C. 2118.

WAR DIARY
INTELLIGENCE SUMMARY.
(Erase heading not required.)

Instructions regarding War Diaries and Intelligence Summaries are contained in F. S. Regs., Part II, and the Staff Manual respectively. Title pages will be prepared in manuscript.

Hour, Date, Place.	Summary of Events and Information.	Remarks and references to Appendices.
EMBREVILLE. Jan 10th 1916	Dismounted route march for Squadrons. Maj Evans proceeded to ABBEVILLE in car and arranged for refixing of roofs in MOYENVILLE cantin with French authorities, arranged for journey up to Y with us a new ground at CHAUSSOY. Road work continued. Lt Reid Kerr proceeded on leave.	
" 11th "	Road work and Canadian training continued.	
" 12th "	Squadron paraded full strength at 11.30 am at COURTIEUX for inspection by Corps Commander, who was pleased with the turnouts of men. He remarked that many drivers looked unhappy and that the squadron was not as cheerful as usual. All should we is should be. Lt Reid Kerr went on leave.	
" 13th "	Capt Gresswell returned from leave. Lt Cameron with 12 men + 9 troop horses to BUFFLES to open up a new ground at CHAUSSOY and to look after roads in the bivouac areas. Road work and Canadian training continued.	
" 14th "	Maj Evans proceeded on leave. Capt Gresswell proceeded in a car to CHAUSSOY to visit the new quarry. Work in progress on the opening up of the quarry, together with approach roads and bridge across a stream. The 6th Cavalry Brigade to use as a working party. Road work and Canadian training continued. Drainage work on roads most urgently looking it, was intimated to Brigade, to be commenced at once.	
" 15th "	Road work and Canadian training continued.	
" 16th "	Road work + grenadier training continued. Capt Gresswell inspects the road BUIGNY – HOCQUCLUS.	

Army Form C. 2118.

WAR DIARY
INTELLIGENCE SUMMARY.
(Erase heading not required.)

Instructions regarding War Diaries and Intelligence Summaries are contained in F. S. Regs., Part II, and the Staff Manual respectively. Title pages will be prepared in manuscript.

Hour, Date, Place.		Summary of Events and Information.	Remarks and references to Appendices.
EMBREVILLE	Jan 17th 1916.	Grenadier Training and road work continued.	EJ.S
	18	Rifle Inspection by Armourer 8th D.Gs. Road work and grenadier training continues. Work commenced on the BUIGNY - HOCQUNCOURT road.	EJ.S
	19	Capt Grenwell took half the Squadron in Troop Drill; road work and grenadier training continued.	EJ.S
	20	Inspection of road work by A.D. + Q.M.G. 1st I.C.D. and Capt Grenwell. Regiments are employed in cutting catch water drains, and levelling banks thrown forwards on opening up the Quarry at CHAUSSOY. Grenadier training continues.	EJ.S
	21	Road work and grenadier training continues.	EJ.S
	22	Do.	EJ.S
	23	Do. Maj Evans returned from leave. Exercise & road work. Men given half holiday. Officers attended a lecture at Corps HQ on "Artillery at LOOS".	EJ.S
	24	This trench warfare class commenced. Maj Evans lectures on General principles and details of trenches in running. Capt Grenwell lectured on tools & materials. Capt Ross Kerr returned from leave. Road work continued. Route march & troops drill under the Regimental, went to work.	EJ.S
	25th	Capt Grenwell lectured on revetments and wire entanglements. Maj Evans on drainage. Capt Ross Kerr on obstacles. N.C.Os & Indians employed in revetting. Road work continued.	EJ.S
	26th	Capt Grenwell lectured on M.G. Emplacements & to N.Cos. Maj Evans lectured on construction of dugouts. Capt Ross Kerr lectured on listening posts sap-heads and saps. Also loopholes & sandbag parapets. Long-known small arm leave	EJ.S

Army Form O. 2118.

WAR DIARY

INTELLIGENCE SUMMARY.

(Erase heading not required.)

Instructions regarding War Diaries and Intelligence Summaries are contained in F. S. Regs., Part II, and the Staff Manual respectively. Title pages will be prepared in manuscript.

Hour, Date, Place.	Summary of Events and Information.	Remarks and references to Appendices.
EMBREVILLE. Jan 27 1916	Maj Evans lectured on laying out trenches and working parties. Capt Cresswell on Grenades Etc. 2nd Lieut Charlton R.F.A. lectured on operations of artillery co-operation, and Maj Evans on defence of wood. Road work continued.	W.E.
" 28 "	Capt Ross'es Kemp lectured on Explosives and Demolitions. Maj Evans on "attacks & counter-attacks". Class ended in afternoon. Road work continued.	W.E.
" 29 "	Maj Evans inspected work in ground in vicinity of CHAUSSOY. Men now engaged in working on trenches under Lt Gauvain. New war game at CHAUSSOY. Road work continued. Exercises and roadwork.	W.E.
" 30 "	Maj Evans & Capt Cresswell visited 4th Div area to find out about work to be done by trench digging party. Road work continued. Also filling in of practice trenches.	W.E.
" 31 "		W.E.

MAJOR, R.E.
O.C. 1st INDIAN FIELD SQUADRON, R.E.
1st INDIAN CAVALRY DIVISION.

SERIAL NO. 118.

Confidential

War Diary

of

1st Indian Field Squadron R.E.

FROM 1st February 1916 TO 29th February 1916

Army Form C. 2118.

WAR DIARY
or
INTELLIGENCE SUMMARY.
(Erase heading not required.)

Instructions regarding War Diaries and Intelligence Summaries are contained in F. S. Regs., Part II, and the Staff Manual respectively. Title pages will be prepared in manuscript.

Hour, Date, Place.	Summary of Events and Information.	Remarks and references to Appendices.
EMBREVILLE. Feb 1st 1916	Road work continued. Troop training. Officers attended lecture by Major Warren R.E. on "Battle of Loos."	
2nd	Road work continued & troop training. Maj Evans attended Trench attack scheme by Lucknow Brigade; inspected road work.	
3rd	Road work continued. Remts waved in mounted order.	
4th	Road work continued & Troop training. All branches filled in.	
5th	Road work & Troop training continued. 2Lt Jorgensham returned from leave. 15 horses lent by 8th Cavalry to H.Q. Div to Commission 2nd A Army for riding instruction.	
6th	Troops for riding instruction. Men given half holiday. Capt Chase rejoined from 13th Div Staff.	
7th	Road work continued. Dismounted parts waved with Capt Gaskell. Maj Evans inspected roads. Capt Chase appointed an instructor at 3rd Army School, temporarily.	
8th	Road work & troop training. Capt Chase left for 3rd Army School. Officers attended lecture by a French capt in his experiences on a squadron leader ready in the war.	
9th	Road work continued. Remts waved on scale as for a mounted unit.	
10th	Road work & troop training continued. Officers attended lecture by Brig Gen Home on "Cavalry in early part of war."	
11th	Road work & troop training continued.	
12th	Do. Maj Evans visited 3rd Army School at FLIXECOURT to witness a mounted attack.	
13th	Inspected road work. Half holiday for men.	

WAR DIARY
INTELLIGENCE SUMMARY
(Erase heading not required.)

Army Form C. 2118.

Instructions regarding War Diaries and Intelligence Summaries are contained in F. S. Regs., Part II, and the Staff Manual respectively. Title pages will be prepared in manuscript.

Hour, Date, Place.	Summary of Events and Information.	Remarks and references to Appendices.
Feb 14 1916. EMBREVILLE.	Road work continued. B and C Troops set return to reconnoitre crossings over river BRESLE. Maj. V.F. Church Res. of Offrs, 13 Hussars reported his arrival on being attached to the Squadron for supernumerary Sanitary duties; have a stable management.	[initials]
15th —	Road work & Troop Training. Maj Evans inspected road work and interviewed the French Engineers in ABBEVILLE.	[initials]
16th —	Road work & Troop Training. Maj Evans interviewed French road Engineers in E.V.	[initials]
17th —	Road work & troop training. Capt Cumwell with 27 other ranks, 9 horses, 1 G.S. wagon returned at 3 pm with stopping party. 3rd storing team British regiments in Corps to stay on 7th Corps line. Billeting at BUS. LES ARTOIS. Capt Railton with 29 other ranks, 9 horses, 1 G.S. and 1 G.S. wagon entrained at Saeurs Tin with an advance party for work on 17th Corps Line. Billeting at FORCEVILLE.	[initials]
18th —	Road work & troop training. Lieut Farquharson blew up mines failed Grenades for 36th Horse.	[initials]
19th —	Maj Evans inspected road work. Troop training.	[initials]
20th —	Holy holiday granted troops. Only Reveille in running. A troop carrying Cash with leavings & trn training visited Canadian & Troop Road work & Troop training.	[initials]
21st —	Sunday.	[initials]
22nd —	Lt Farquharson with 33 other ranks, 3 horses, G.S. wagon & tool cart 7 B troop marched to FLIXECOURT for work at 3rd Army behind the Maj Evans inspected 3rd Army Schools in company with other commanding officers of the Squadrons.	[initials]
23rd —	Owing to heavy road work discontinued. Except for A Troop, who are employed on certain small jobs, only Supplying means were at headquarters to exercise horses.	[initials]
24th —		[initials]

Army Form C. 2118.

WAR DIARY
or
INTELLIGENCE SUMMARY.

(Erase heading not required.)

Instructions regarding War Diaries and Intelligence Summaries are contained in F. S. Regs., Part II, and the Staff Manual respectively. Title pages will be prepared in manuscript.

Hour, Date, Place.	Summary of Events and Information.	Remarks and references to Appendices.
Feb 25 1916 EMBREVILLE	Road work interrupted by snow. 2nd Corourum injured to 13th Corps for temporary duty.	
26 —	Heavy snow, brevier only.	
27 —	Half holiday for men. Maj Browne went to inspect C & X troops but car stuck twice in snowdrifts & he was unable to reach them.	
28 —	Thaw scheme put in to operation by which ni corner lines etc were along roads. Horses covered in frills. All work stopped	
29 —	Thaw scheme continued. Informed that RE Corourum no attached to officer of C.E. XIII Corps as personal assistant	

W. Browne
MAJOR, R.E.
O.C. 1ST INDIAN FIELD SQUADRON, R.E.
1ST INDIAN CAVALRY DIVISION.

SERIAL NO. 148.

Confidential

War Diary

of

1st Indian Field Squadron, R.E.

FROM 1st March 1916 TO 31st March 1916.

Army Form C. 2118.

WAR DIARY
or
INTELLIGENCE SUMMARY.
(Erase heading not required.)

Instructions regarding War Diaries and Intelligence Summaries are contained in F.S. Regs., Part II, and the Staff Manual respectively. Title pages will be prepared in manuscript.

Hour, Date, Place.	Summary of Events and Information.	Remarks and references to Appendices.
March 1st 1916 EMBREVILLE	Three squadron drill in squadron. Maj Brown & Church inspected riding drill, stables & horses of Canadian Field Troops. Inspected work on gunnery and rockets.	
2nd " "	All work on roads except BEAUCHAMPS – WOINCOURT stopped. Route march for A troop and bridging train.	
3rd " "	Major Brown inspected troops on detachment and work in hand. C troop at BUS in Corps Line with 48th Div; D troop at FORCEVILLE on Corps Line with 36th Div; B troop at FLIXECOURT with 3rd Army School	
4th " "	Exercise only. Half holiday	
5th " "	Very bad weather. Exercise only	
6th " "	Horses from Canadians returned. A troop in troop drill.	
7th " "	Instructed & Reserves & mining drill. A troop in troop drill. D Troop, less OC & transport returned by Bus from FORCEVILLE, leaving Corps Cavalry Communication squadron from 13th Corps	
8th " "	Maj Brown & Lt Gammon attended Staff ride: tactical scheme cunning of river BRESLE. Route march for A troop and Bridging Train. B troop checking equipment. Corps Staff abolished. 1st	
9th " "	Div placed directly under 3rd Army	
10th " "	Conference at Div HQ on various points. A & B troops in troop drill.	
11th " "	B troop returned from FLIXECOURT by route march and rest of D troop by route march from FORCEVILLE. Half holiday.	
12th " "	Exercise only in troop drill. B & D troops checking equipment	
13th " "	A troop in troop drill.	
14th " "	A troop sent to MAISNIERES to assist Sialkot Brigade in a scheme including the demolition of a railway junction. B & D troops holding practice to take over GAMACHES	
15th " "	Troop training.	

Army Form C. 2118.

WAR DIARY
or
INTELLIGENCE SUMMARY.
(Erase heading not required.)

Instructions regarding War Diaries and Intelligence Summaries are contained in F. S. Regs., Part II, and the Staff Manual respectively. Title pages will be prepared in manuscript.

Hour, Date, Place.	Summary of Events and Information.	Remarks and references to Appendices.
March 16 1916. EMBREVILLE.	A troop practised bridging at BOUVAINCOURT. B & D carried out an intercommunication scheme across R. BRESLE.	
17 —	All officers attended a divisional staff ride; returned same evening.	
18 —	Defence of around S of BRESLE. D troop in troop drill. RHA tried a section of squadron bridging equipment, which it is hoped they should carry themselves to cross trenches during an attack. Troop training.	
19 —	Reconnaissance only; half holiday.	
20 —	Lt Cameron visited AUXI-LE-CHATEAU to see about work.	
21 —	Course for 3rd Army School. D troop bridging at BOUVAINCOURT. Remainder at troop drill.	
— —	C troop (Capt Cunwell, 23 other ranks) returned from 48th Div by train and lorry; transport marching. Lt Cameron & 2/Lt R went in lorry to 3rd Army School at AUXI-LE-CHATEAU. B and D troops employed in between for demolishing railway bridges over BRESLE and preparing bridge defences. Capt Cunwell went in command.	
22 —	Troop training. Prepared to embrace to clarity view Capt Chanis, temporary to RE reported to squadron. 30 field Coy R.E.	
23 —	Troop training.	
24/25 —	Troop Training.	
25/26 —	Troop Training and preparing for moving billets.	
26/27 —	"B" Squadron marched to Oneux and billeted the night there en route to Auxi-le-Chateau. Maj Sweeny: Commanded the Column consisting of Bde? Troops. Capt Robertson with the Indirection advanced went on ahead to do the billeting.	
27 — Oneux.	The Squadron marched to their new billeting area at Auxi-le-Chateau; Lt Farquharson went on ahead to do the billeting. Villa Germain with 22.0.R rejoined the Squadron on arrival.	

Army Form C. 2118.

WAR DIARY
INTELLIGENCE SUMMARY
(Erase heading not required.)

Instructions regarding War Diaries and Intelligence Summaries are contained in F. S. Regs., Part II, and the Staff Manual respectively. Title pages will be prepared in manuscript.

Hour, Date, Place.	Summary of Events and Information.	Remarks and references to Appendices.
March 28th 1916 Auxi-le-Chateau	Troop Training. Reconnaitre investigated all damage done by French troops to area occupied by the Squadron. 2/Lt Grammer with 24 Sappers is placed at the disposal of the 3rd Army School.	JAQ
" 29th " "	Troop Training. Strength of party attached to 3rd Army School increased from 24 to 28 Sappers. Maj Brown went on leave. Capt Rait-Kerr RE assumed Command of the Squadron pending Capt Grisewood's return from leave.	JAQ
" 30th " "	C troop did Troop drill under Major Church; B Troop bridging on the R. Authie S.E of Vitz; remainder exercise.	JAQ
" 31st " "	Soffer walker promoted to 2 Lt and left the Squadron to join the 6th Northamptonshire Regt. C & D troops did Bridging S.E of Vitz under 2 Lt Bennett; remainder exercise.	JAQ

JA Farquharson Lt
A/Cpt 4/4/16

War Diary
of
1st Ind. Field Sqr. RE
1st Ind Cav Divn
March 1916

SERIAL NO. 148.

Confidential

War Diary

of

1st Indian Field Squadron, R.E.

FROM 1st April 1916 TO 30th April 1916.

WAR DIARY
INTELLIGENCE SUMMARY.
(Erase heading not required.)

Army Form C. 2118.

Hour, Date, Place.	Summary of Events and Information.	Remarks and references to Appendices.
AUXI-LE-CHATEAU. April 1st 1916.	Troop training. Lt Bennett investigated water-supply. 29th Lancers Capt Gould returned from leave.	
" " 2	Half holiday. Doctor only. Capt Roie Rew went on leave. Lt Bennett surveyed trenches at ST RIQUIER (French training ground)	
" " 3	Troop training. C troop on drill.	
" " 4	Troop training.	
" " 5	Troop training. B troop on mining drill.	
" " 6	Troop training. C & S troop training. B on mining drill.	
" " 7	Troop training. Lt Bennett & Coy surveyed ST RIQUIER trenches.	
" " 8	Maj Evans returned from leave.	
" " 9	Troop training. C troop on drill.	
" " 10	Half holiday. Exercise only.	
" " 11	8 Troops on drill. Lt Farquharson on leaving up to 4.9 unemployed & idle French shell, unusing a fuse-up for 17 horses, and electric lighting installation for the Lancers. Remainder on work for Army School. Lt Warwick went on leave.	
" " 12	C troop on drill. Lt Bennett & 2 sappers went to construct down-for 29 Lancers at FONTAINE. Major Evans inspected work for Army School & Rifle Brigade. Lt Goodman went on leave	
" " 13	Heavy rain. B troop preparing for musketry. Rest on Army School work. Leave stopped as all men needed. 2 troops on drill, rest on Army School work in morning. Nearly all sappers on Army School work in morning, in afternoon attended flammenwerfer demonstration with Minor Brigade	
" " 14	2 Troops on drill, remainder on Army School work. Maj Evans went on to see C.&. 3rd Army about work for Division.	
" " 15	Half holiday. Exercise & work for Army School in morning.	
" " 16	1 Troop on drill, 1 troop on musketry, rest on Army School work.	
" " 17	Maj Evans attended staff ride (Divisional) at ST RIQUIER.	

Army Form C. 2118.

WAR DIARY
INTELLIGENCE SUMMARY.

(Erase heading not required.)

Instructions regarding War Diaries and Intelligence Summaries are contained in F.S. Regs., Part II, and the Staff Manual respectively. Title pages will be prepared in manuscript.

Hour, Date, Place.	Summary of Events and Information.	Remarks and references to Appendices.
AUXI LE CHATEAU. April 18. 1916.	1 Troop on drill. Rest on exercise and Army School work. Very wet. Maj Evans & Lieut Farquharson went to VACQUERIETTE to see about work required for Divisional School.	WA
" 19 "	Lieuts Farquharson & Bennett with 63 other ranks and 6 horses left for VACQUERIETTE for work on Divisional School, leaving A, B, C troops with only 1 non. to 3 non., D troop employed on Army School.	WA
" 20 "	Maj Evans inspected work at VACQUERIETTE, consisting of 2 miles of trenches, 2 huts, a range and tables, fences, wire troughs etc.	WA
" 21st "	Troops on Army School work. A, B, C on Div School work.	WA
" 22 "	Heavy rain. Trenches at VACQUERIETTE reported to have fallen in; arrangements made for rivetting. Maj Evans attended conference at Div H.Q.	WA
" 23rd "	Hours ceased owing to legend as heavy rain had made field unworkable. Maj Evans inspected work at VACQUERIETTE.	WA
" 24th "	Work continued as before. Lawn games. Capt Rair Ken proceeded on leave.	WA
" 25th "	Work continued as before. Capt Warwick returned from leave. Lt Farquharson with A & B Troops returned from VACQUERIETTE.	WA
" 26th "	Camp to Bennett in charge with C troop. Major Evans attended Staff Ride with Div and Brigade Staffs under Gen Gough.	WA
" 27th "	A & B troops employed on sanitation work. D troop on Army School, C troop on Div School. Capt Warwick transferred to No 19 Casualty Clearing Station at DOULLENS. Major Evans attended continuation of Staff Ride under Gen Gough.	WA
" 28 "	A troop on drill. B troop troop training. D troop Army School & C troop Div School work. Lt Phillips RAMC joined the Squadron.	WA
" 29 "	A troop drill, B troop training, D Army School work. C troop under Lt Bennett returned from VACQUERIETTE.	WA
" 30 "	Half holiday. Troops ordinal troops officers for inspection. Maj Evans attended conference at Div H.Q.	WA

W.H. Evans
Major R.E.
O.C. 1st Div Field Squadron R.E.
1st Can Div.
30/4/16.

War Diary.
1st Indian Field
Squadron
R.E.

1st Indi: Cav. Divn

April — 1916

SERIAL NO. 148.

Confidential

War Diary

of

1st Indian Field Squadron, R.E.

FROM 1st May 1916 TO 31st May 1916.

Army Form C. 2118.

WAR DIARY
INTELLIGENCE SUMMARY.
(Erase heading not required.)

Instructions regarding War Diaries and Intelligence Summaries are contained in F. S. Regs., Part II, and the Staff Manual respectively. Title pages will be prepared in manuscript.

1st INDIAN FIELD SQUADRON · 1st INDIAN CAVALRY DIVISION
No. .... Date ....

Hour, Date, Place.	Summary of Events and Information.	Remarks and references to Appendices.
HANCHY. 1916. May 1st	Troops complete with all officers marched to ST RIQUIER. Training also billeting at HANCHY. Bridging Train and headquarters with division reinforcements remained at AUXI. Le Longhorn blew up a 6" shell found at GUESCHART. Squadron still in training area in afternoon. Maj. Broun attended conference at Div HQ at 5 p.m.	[sig]
2nd	Squadron moved at 8 am to function of xroads at CRAMONT. B troop ordered to Siollets Bridge in vicinity of GAPENNES. A troop ordered to Lackman Bridge. Remainder in reserve helping RHA near trenches. No wheels taken.	[sig]
3rd	Squadron marched 7.30 A to function of xroads between ARGENT VILLERS and GAPENNES. B troop ordered to Siollet bridge for attack on ONEUX. Remainder in reserve. No wheels taken.	[sig]
4th	Squadron marched 7.45 am to position of concentration of HEIRMONT: wheels taken and left in HEIRMONT with A Echelon of Brigade. B troop attacked to Siollet Bridge to attack: remainder moved to position of Indian Cavalry in reserve. Gen Gough, Gen Reserve Corps, was directing the field day.	[sig]
5th	No divisional training. Squadron paraded at 8 am with wheels and proceeded to training ground for Squadron drill. Officers and NCOs looked over reported defences of ONEUX village, while horses grazed. Greasing again in afternoon. Lt Farquharson went on leave, Squadron under Capt Cromwell.	[sig]
6th	At AUXI LE CHATEAU. Major Broun attended divisional manoeuvres in training area, Capt Reid Kerr returned from leave appointed instructor in Military Engineering at 3rd Army School.	[sig]
7th	Half holiday, for men. Battery arranged for whole squadron	[sig]
8th	A troop on drill. 2 on army school work. Blew up 32 French shells in afternoon.	[sig]

AUXI-LE-CHATEAU

Army Form C. 2118.

WAR DIARY
or
INTELLIGENCE SUMMARY.
(Erase heading not required.)

Instructions regarding War Diaries and Intelligence Summaries are contained in F. S. Regs., Part II, and the Staff Manual respectively. Title pages will be prepared in manuscript.

Hour, Date, Place.	Summary of Events and Information.	Remarks and references to Appendices.
AUXI-LE-CHATEAU. May 9th 1916	Troop training. Capt Gamwell sent forward as billeting officer. Maj Evans attended conference at Div headquarters. Maj Church went on leave.	CWE
" 10th	Sqdrn marched at 9.45 am to LIENCOURT arriving 3.30 pm. Maj Evans commanded column of Sir Troop. Capt Raikes left behind in AUXI-LE-CHATEAU with an instructor. 3rd Army School with a detachment of 22 men, 9 horses, 1 cookcart.	CWE
LIENCOURT " 11th	Troop employed in reconnaissance work in new area.	CWE
" 12th	Sits. All lines inspected by veterinary officer in afternoon.	CWE
" 13th	Troop training. Maj Evans visited C.E. & 61st Corps, Capt Phillips with lance.	CWE
" 14th	Maj Evans inspected structures left by 54th Div in our area.	CWE
" 15th	Visited C.E. again. Arrangts for trucks for horse standings. Equipment of troops checked by C.O. Rejointing of looseways and boots begun.	CWE
" 16th	Maj Evans inspected structures in div area again. Troop training.	CWE
" 17th	Sqdrn employed on village defences scheme. Maj Evans attended conference at Div H.Q. Divisional places on 4 hours notice to move. Officers and NCOs studied defences of AMBRINES.	CWE
" 18th	Capt Gamwell taught Sicilley Brigade wire cutting.	CWE
" 19th / 20th	Officers and NCOs studied defences of DENIER in detail. Maj Church returned from leave. Officers and NCOs studied defences of MAGNICOURT in detail. Maj Evans inspected GIVENCHY LE NOBLE with G.O.C. & staff with view of establishing a Divisional school there.	CWE
" 21st	Half holiday for men. Work in ??? etc for Div school commenced.	CWE
" 22nd	Troop training. Maj Evans went through defences of MAGNICOURT for 6 cavalry. Gens Kadar and Maxwell Purnell. Pt Bennett and 9 other ranks proceed to VACQUERIETTE as motor bus to darmside Div School	CWE

Army Form C. 2118.

WAR DIARY
or
INTELLIGENCE SUMMARY.

(Erase heading not required.)

Instructions regarding War Diaries and Intelligence Summaries are contained in F.S. Regs., Part II, and the Staff Manual respectively. Title pages will be prepared in manuscript.

Hour, Date, Place.	Summary of Events and Information.	Remarks and references to Appendices.
LIENCOURT. May 23rd 1916.	Maj Evans went through defences of AMBRINES with 19 Lancers, also studied defences of BEAUDRICOURT. Troops returned to Phillip.	
" 24 "	Maj Evans went through defences of DENIER with 17 Lancers. Troop training. Conference subsequently on feasibility for Squadron indicated 36 hours wine in defences of town. Capt Grenwell drill in off town work.	
" 25 "	Maj Evans went through defences of BEAUDRICOURT for Mhow Brigade. Capt Grenwell instructed 19 Lancers in bivouac in billets. Troop training.	
" 26 "	Maj Evans went to Dehzes situations in rapid winning. Capt helmet drill in off town work. Sqdn school furnished Carpenters in Sqn school.	
" 27 "	Maj Evans instructed 19 Lancers in defence of AMBRINES, in driving troops for moving etc. Capt Grenwell & C troop completed trenches in defence of Jumicourt for Mhow Brigade. Lt Burnett instructing 17 Lancers actually posted in tanks. Lt Burnett act.	
LIGNEUREUIL.	" "	
" 28 "	with most of 19 Lancers actually posted in tanks & handed over. Lt Burnett meets school at GIVENCHY completed & handed over. Sqn school.	
" 29 "	Cap Lut II continued work to army school in action. Cpl dug well. Maj. Evans & Capt Grenwell inspected Cpls log N & S Acer. A & B troops attending trench Lt Burnett continued work in Sqn school. Capt Grenwell did Sqdn for Cavalry reinforcements Lucknow Brigade.	
" 30 "	Sixty Lucknow Brigade. Capt Grenwell with B troop assisted 17 Lancers in defence of DENIER. Lt Cameron with A troop assisted 6 Cav. in defence of MAGNICOURT. Troops were with Army school at AUX-LE-CHATEAU. Troop. Maj Evans continued work all Sqn school.	
" 31 "	Sqdn took part in Divisional holiday. Lt Cameron with A troop attached to Mhow Brigade ad demolished bridges over R CANCHE, for Fergusson with B troop attached to Lucknow Brigade. Remainder in reserve.	

O.C. 1st INDIAN FIELD SQUADRON, R.E.

MAJOR, R.E.
1st INDIAN CAVALRY DIVISION.

WAR DIARY
of

1st INDIAN FIELD SQUADRON — 1st INDIAN CAVALRY DIVISION
Date: MAY 1916.

SERIAL NO. 148.

Confidential
War Diary
of

1st Indian Field Squadron, R.E.

FROM 1st June 1916 TO 30th June 1916

Army Form C. 2118.

WAR DIARY
or
INTELLIGENCE SUMMARY.
(Erase heading not required.)

Instructions regarding War Diaries and Intelligence Summaries are contained in F. S. Regs., Part II, and the Staff Manual respectively. Title pages will be prepared in manuscript.

Hour, Date, Place.	Summary of Events and Information.	Remarks and references to Appendices.
LIENCOURT. June 1st 1916 2nd 1916	Troop training. Men at 3rd Army School relieved Squadron parade and with moved to 3SL HAMEAU. Practical chance from front wheels to rock.	
3rd	A troop Musketry. B troop practice in transfer to packs. C troop battle outpost.	
	by Bennett with 10 men proceeded to ARRAS to contact observation posts for D battery R.H.A. C troop R.H.A. Divisional school completed. Maj Evans inspected work being done on standings by units. Capt Gardell proceeded on leave.	
4th	Half holiday for men. Dy Doryphorn took 17 NCOs & men, 18 horses, mules & harnesses to MARSEVIL to continue level parts for R.H.A brigade. Dy Doryphorn returned, handing over to Dy Bennett. ARRAS. Maj Evans learnt no extension of IVERGNY in morning and B013. DE FAYE in afternoon & men sent to join school for training in Hutchins work & knotting.	
5th	Maj Evans with B troop went to commence & B troop wanted in defence of IVERGNY. Remainder troop training.	
6th	IVERGNY. Remainder troop training. Maj Evans with 1st Gunmonn & A troop carried out defence by 6th Dragoons of IVERGNY. Remainder troop training.	
7th	A troop battle. C troop. B troop musketry training. Gunnies training in afternoon with live bombs. Maj Evans inspected detachment in ARRAS.	
8th	Maj Evans with B troop & Dy Doryphorn defended IVERGNY for 38th C 9H. A troop with 1st Gunmonn united in crossing at CANCHE river by 17th Lancers.	
9th 10	A troop musketry. B troop on work for Div School. A troop on harness in getting horses over river. Maj Evans attended staff ride conducted by Gore Gunnel's Corft in Allerby prenely.	
11th 12th	Half holiday for men. Exercise only A troop on infantry in getting horses over river. B in new establishment. copy Dr Bennett & party returns from ARRAS.	

Army Form C. 2118.

WAR DIARY
INTELLIGENCE SUMMARY.
(Erase heading not required.)

Instructions regarding War Diaries and Intelligence Summaries are contained in F.S. Regs., Part II, and the Staff Manual respectively. Title pages will be prepared in manuscript.

Hour, Date, Place.		Summary of Events and Information.	Remarks and references to Appendices.
LIENCOURT. June 13th 1916 – 17	–	Very wet. Exercise only. No training possible. Troop training. Capt Grenvill returned from & Lt Bennett proceeded on leave. Maj Evans inspected work done by detachment C troop for R.H.A. Brigade near MARŒUIL and arranged for their relief by B troop.	Sgt
14th	–	Troop training. Lt Longbourne with 20 other ranks proceeded to BRIGADE HEAD QRS for 24 hours and 9 other ranks returned to work.	WE.
15	–	RHA Brigade Headqrs moved to	W.E
16		Troop training. A troop Lining.	
17		Troop training. Maj Evans attended divisional Staff ride.	WE
18		Half holiday. Exercise only.	
19th		Major Evans went on leave. Exercise in morning. Practice in crossing wet canvas + tarpaulin rafts. Capt Grenvill instructs sqn L.	HEF
20th		in raft using. Party (apt of C troop) doing School stores arrive near MARŒUIL. Entrenchments in Suzanne wood.	
21st		Exercise in morning. C+D + Hd squadron. Capt Grenvill attack & reconnaissance work. MAROEUIL with Staff, 1st C.D. and also inspected Lt Longbourne letter in the training. Got infected concrete tanks wet. Some references.	HEF
22nd		Troop training + Exercise. Capt Grenvill reconnoiters forming up places with Staff Captain, Indian Cav Bde.	HEF
23rd		Troop on rate march. Conference of O.C's at Div HQrs.	HEF
24th		Troop training + Exercise.	HEF
25th		Half holiday. Exercise only.	HEF
26th		Squadron rate march – practised changing to pack.	HEF
27th		Exercise only – Major Evans returns from leave.	HEF

Army Form C. 2118.

WAR DIARY
or
INTELLIGENCE SUMMARY.
(Erase heading not required.)

Instructions regarding War Diaries and Intelligence Summaries are contained in F. S. Regs., Part II, and the Staff Manual respectively. Title pages will be prepared in manuscript.

Hour, Date, Place.	Summary of Events and Information.	Remarks and references to Appendices.
LIENCOURT Aug 28th 1916	Troop Training. Capt Gamwell visited new billeting area to be about water supply for division. Lt Farquharson with 21 men of B troop returned from R H A Brigade	*sgd*
" 29 "	Troop training and Smoke helmet drill. Capt Gamwell with a small party went on to concentration area near BOULLENS.	*sgd*
" 30 "	Marched to concentration area at LE MARAIS SEC nr outskirts of BOULLENS.	*sgd*

[signature]

Major pl
OC 1st m Indian Field Squadron
1st m Indian Cavalry Division

30/6/16.

War Diary.

1st Indian Field Squadron
1st Indian Division

June 1916

SERIAL NO. 148.

Confidential

War Diary

of

1st Indian Field Squadron R.E.

FROM 1st July 1916 TO 31st July 1916.

WAR DIARY / INTELLIGENCE SUMMARY

Army Form C. 2118

Place	Date	Hour	Summary of Events and Information	Remarks and references to Appendices
DOULLENS	July 1/9?	—	Troops employed on carrying horses over river in morning and smoke helmet drill in afternoon. G.O.C. saw horses. Placed at 3 hours notice to move.	ref
AUXI-LE-CHATEAU	2nd	—	River crossing & smoke helmet drill. Division moved at very short notice to AUXI-LE-CHATEAU. Billeting squadron in RUE D'ABBEVILLE. Hotchkiss on saddle allotted to Sqn. Cav.	ref
	3rd	—	Fitting into new area as smoke helmet drill. Reinforcements returned.	ref
	4th	—	A troop min. cunning. Revolver practising charge to pack. Pack saddle made for H.Q.	ref
	5th	—	A troop & C troop with Lucknow Brigade. Horses, & arms & kits Z. 1. Troop 29 and T. troop 36 taken across by tackle - wetted & bought back by saddle rope. C Troop took similar across also. D Troop numerical practice with M.O. B Troop numerical refreshments. C on alberry	ref
	6th	—	A troop with wood & charging to back. B & D on river crossing refreshments.	ref
	7th	—	Troop in river carrying experiments. Very heavy rain. 3 mule saddles attached for 6 tanks on A.H.T. Coy wagons.	ref
	8th	—	Cav. + 8 loop brolls made for 6 Sqns for Hotchkiss equipments. A troop worked with Lucknow Brigade waking bridge on CANAL DE FROHEN-LE-GRAND with 6-8 wagon bodies. C bridging. B & D on ladders etc. Here in B troop tupla in by cunning river. 2nd Coy. Bolton nearly drowned: rescued by sappers myself, Breton, Dickson & Sm Powell.	ref
	9th	—	Half holiday. Exercising only in morning.	ref
	10th	—	C & D troops worked with Hann Brigade crossing lines never by tackle and returning by cable & small boat carried in saddle.	ref
	11th	—	Saddles up, Kits & men taken over by cable. A bridging expert. Put in shavonotic numb.	ref
	12th	—	B troop drill & jumping. C & D bridging.	ref
	13th	—	A troop drill. B C & D bridging.	ref
	14th	—	A troop river reconnaissance. B & D Bridging. C troop drill. Squadron marched to MEZEROLLES and constructed W. 108 foot span in	ref
	15th	—	3r/4 hours.	ref
	16th	—	Maj. Rean + 3 other offs. visited trenches between FRICOURT and MAMETZ. Troops on Maj Kent's station. Tanks ren FRICOURT again to study refrain needed to cav cavalry over trenches. Exercise only for squadron & half holiday	ref

WAR DIARY / INTELLIGENCE SUMMARY

Army Form C. 2118

(1st Indian Field Squadron, 1st Indian Cavalry Division stamp)

Place	Date	Hour	Summary of Events and Information	Remarks and references to Appendices
AUXI LE CHATEAU	July 17, 1916		Troops in cleaning wagons, sharpening tools. A troop cutting wagons over river crossing bridges.	
"	18 "		Squadron marched to River CANCHE and carried out river reconnaissance, making bridges and rebuilding demolished ones.	
AGNIERES	19 "		Division moved to 17 Corps area, Field Squadron moved to AGNIERES near AUBIGNY. Maj Evans went on advance party to see staff of 60th Div.	
"	20 "		2 trades to work for 60th Div. Cpl Gaswell & 1 sapping work to La Clinie. Maj Evans & 3 other officers inspected a took over work to be done. Cavalry with 3 troops (54 sapping) marched to ANZIN ST AUBIN in XVII Corps. RFA Gun emplacements work directly with 3 troops at EMPIRE and until; men employing in day for work at EMPIRE as not being done by 3 troops at EMPIRE wait until; men employing. Maj Evans inspected work at taggering trenches.	
"	21 "		1 house work by day and 1 by night. Ordered treveller houseft and employing trenches; 1 house work as assistant to Lt Turner, 60 Div, in charge at Bennett, proceeded to MAROEUIL to work as assistant to Lt Turner.	
"	22 "		Sir Inspected work on RA Gun Emplacements work now commenced. Arranged a truck for transport and despatches a wagon & team to MAROEUIL for work. 28 large flags made up for Div training area.	
"	23 " 24 "		Troops commenced on watersupply for VILLERS CHATEL. Maj Evans inspected Cpl Gaswell work & ran emplacements at battery 8.3, ready for construction on Cpl Gaswell work & wire emplacements. 2nd ready for concrete. Arrangements for materials for materials, water supply installation at VILLERS CHATEL.	
"	25 "		CRA passed cement. Troops inspected work at EMPIRE satisfactorily. Arranged about making dugouts carrying for KSGs in NEUVILLE ST VAAST. Arranged air culps through BRAY and ECOIVRES for materials. Co proceeds on VILLERS CHATEL satisfactorily.	
"	26 "		Maj Evans inspected work near ANZIN; Inspection of cisterns began in one emplacement: 5 ready for concrete. Arrangements for supply of materials. New sanitation work satisfactory, yet. watersupply installation at VILLERS CHATEL completed. 2 men proceed to work A & Q batteries for emplacement work and 6 to NEUVILLE ST VAAST for dugouts.	

Army Form C. 2118

WAR DIARY
or
INTELLIGENCE SUMMARY

(Erase heading not required)

Instructions regarding War Diaries and Intelligence Summaries are contained in F.S. Regs., Part II. and the Staff Manual respectively. Title Pages will be prepared in manuscript.

1st JODHPUR FIELD SQUADRON
1st INDIAN CAVALRY DIVISION

Place	Date	Hour	Summary of Events and Information	Remarks and references to Appendices
AGNIERES	July 27 1916	-	Maj Evans inspected waterworks in use for 1/908. Toughs & pumps erected at SAVY; 6 wells put in hand in shed in BETHONSART. Both pumps in shed at CAMBLIGNEUL. Duration of tanks & toughs complete at VILLERS CHATEL. Capt Grenvell left for Beaufort. 154. 7/8 Coy in command. Capt Raid Ran rejoined from this army school. Jangubar wa slightly wounded by shrapnel in shoulder 11 June 26th when shooting for work on EMPIRE redoubt from BETHUNE road.	[sig]
-	28	-	Maj Evans inspects work on EMPIRE redoubt with C.I. XVII Corps who seems well. Capt Raid Ran pressed friestly modes along PYLONES trench to ANZIN to take charge of work there.	[sig]
-	29	-	Maj Evans inspects work at ANZIN; all emplacements nearly ready for cement; (gauze erected & cementing in hand, in some leaves half erected. Material supply and transport runs smoothly.	[sig]
-	30	-	Maj Evans inspects work at EMPIRE Redoubt: and progress especially in mining. 20 men from Jodhpur Lancers been added to working party at ANZIN wy z, the added would attaches increased by 6 sappers. Party at EMPIRE	[sig]
-	31st	-	Maj Evans inspects work at ANZIN. 12 SAC men (6 to 5th) now attaches at ANZIN for work, also 11 of MAROEUIL for breaking up way sweeping wounded (6-12) of battery A.300, and pigeons 6 sappers detaches to this Army School for work, divisions linning to ARRAS — 1/1.6.F for course of instruction of Jominy. Drainage at ANZIN relieved.	[sig]

[signature]
Major R.E.
Comdg 1st Jodhpur
Fd Sqdn
1st Cavalry Div.

1/8/16.

War Diary.

July 1916.

1st Indian Field Squadron — 1st Indian Cavalry Division

SERIAL NO. 148.

Confidential War Diary of

1st Indian Field Squadron, S.C.

FROM 1st August 1916 TO 31st August 1916.

WAR DIARY or **INTELLIGENCE SUMMARY**
(Erase heading not required.)

Army Form C. 2118

Instructions regarding War Diaries and Intelligence Summaries are contained in F. S. Regs., Part II. and the Staff Manual respectively. Title Pages will be prepared in manuscript.

Place	Date	Hour	Summary of Events and Information	Remarks and references to Appendices
AGNIERES	Aug 1st 1916		Waterspply pipe Lukhnow Bridge visited. Temp/Lt J.H. Gardner joined the Squadron from tank.	
	2		Watersupply work at Empires advanced mining finished; new pipe track begun; fair progress on Batty entce; fin steps in PYLONES begun. Saw work of 2 sappers attached to a battery on O.P. and emplacements.	
	3		Fair progress my sappers attached ANZ.I.N. N°1 emplacement A 3rd amt emcts to alms; N°2 emcts to willow nearly done. 2 emplacements B258 begun being trated by Gardner attachd	
	4		to 3/3rd London Fd Coy (6° section) work on right sector. AW H.Q. work finished; huts to 9 interpreters THIEUX tarminated. work continued. Sigual Regument communical Shomys; misling damaged ways sucessfully	
	5		transfer for J. Oliphain Levels. St Berwatt attachs to 1/6 London Coy for work on sapfrey sector At EMPIRE redoubt mining nearly finishd; fair progress in dug outs & new trench.	
	6		Lieu Biggs Rt joined unit from leave. Battery A 3rd N°1 emplacement upper not begun. B258 N°1 connecting com N°s 2 & 3 begins ridge section. New work at LABYRINTHE redoubt.	
	7		emcts. Maj Chicat left on appointment as Commandant ST RIQUIER training centre. 2nd Lt Batten attachs work continued. M de LOGIS OLIVA joined as French interpreter.	
	8		to XVII Corps heavy artillery as Interpreter adviser. work on EMPIRE redoubt fair progress in enettes, new trench and dug outs, mining finished.	
	9		fair progress on concrete emplacements, B Trip moved during night to ARIANE for work on LABYRINTHE redoubt, Lt Bennett joined for assistance to Pargbreven.	
	10		high explosives on LABYRINTHE redoubt. 150 rounds of intermittent bottalim attached for work; 37 to remain at ANZ.I.N. for work in emplacements, remainder	
	11		to live at ARIANE. Work on redoubt continued. Fair progress on redoubt; tunk on South begun (new work); reveting & covering in begun on side begun, the Philips (MC) proceed on leave (interior)	
	12		In unit for NC emplacement cone emplacements complete; 2 emplacements nearly complete; other work in progress. At Pargleren proceed on a further advance.	

Army Form C. 2118

WAR DIARY
or
INTELLIGENCE SUMMARY
(Erase heading not required.)

Instructions regarding War Diaries and Intelligence Summaries are contained in F.S. Regs., Part II. and the Staff Manual respectively. Title Pages will be prepared in manuscript.

Place	Date	Hour	Summary of Events and Information	Remarks and references to Appendices
AGNIERES	Aug 13 1916		Good progress on dugouts and emplacements. Orders issued to provide emplacements unit found, which will take one month to complete.	
	14		Good progress on dugouts and emplacements; certain modifications decided on.	
	15		Good progress on work. 2/Lt Graham joined squadron.	
	16		Good progress on work, inspected by Chief Engineer Third Army.	
	17		Good progress on work. Details of LABYRINTH redoubt settled.	
	18		Scheme for emplacements in hand; work will be finished in 4 or 5 days. Good progress in LABYRINTH redoubt, his work interfered with by demolition galleries.	
	19		Good progress in work.	
	20		Communication trench LABYRINTH redoubt completed. Good progress on dugouts in Corps emplacements. Maj Evans saw G.o.c. Heavy Corps Artillery XVII Corps regarding dugouts for new batteries.	
	21		Sale of 6 emplacements completed; progress in progress. Site for heavy battery dugouts inspected.	
	22		Good progress on LABYRINTH redoubt & emplacements.	
	23		Work commenced on slit trenches for heavy Corps Artillery dugouts: working party 6" & 60pdr Bn longer.	
	24		Good progress in all work. Emplacements at A.300 finally completed.	
	25		Good progress in work.	
	26		New dugouts for R.G.A started in front of MT ST ELOI.	
	27		Good progress in all work.	
	28		Good progress on dugouts for artillery & cutting up of camouflage in front of MT ST ELOI.	
	29		Comp. on emplacements for R.F.A. completed. Work begun on dugouts for R.G.A and	
ANZIN	30		Good progress in LABYRINTH redoubt, wiring begun.	
	31		Work in progress on dugouts for 5 battery positions R.G.A. Good progress in LABYRINTH redoubts	

to Maj. RE
Tubb Squadron
O.C. 1st Indian Field Squadron,
1/9/16. 1st Indian Cavalry Division.

WAR DIARY.

August 1916.

SERIAL NO. 148.

Confidential
War Diary
of

1st Indian Field Squadron, S.E.

FROM 1st September 1916 TO 30th September 1916

Army Form C. 2118

WAR DIARY
INTELLIGENCE SUMMARY
(Erase heading not required.)

Instructions regarding War Diaries and Intelligence Summaries are contained in F.S. Regs., Part II. and the Staff Manual respectively. Title Pages will be prepared in manuscript.

1st INDIAN FIELD SQUADRON
1st INDIAN CAVALRY DIVISION

Place	Date	Hour	Summary of Events and Information	Remarks and references to Appendices
AGNIERES.	Sept 1st 1916.		Squadron concentrated preparatory to move.	
	2nd		Day spent in handing over work, letting Tools and saddlery in order	
	3rd		Squadron marched to CANTELEUX, 21 miles	
CANTELEUX ST RIQUIER.	4th, 5th		Squadron marched to ST RIQUIER, 20 miles	
	5th		Troop Training	
"	6th		Troop & Squadron training.	
"	7th		Squadron training.	
"	8th		Squadron training.	
"	9th		Troop foot in Sir field day. Capt Reid/Kerr interviewed.	R.J.O.K.
"	10th		Troop & Squadron training. Troop training	R.J.O.K.
Occoches	11th		Squadron marched to Occoches 15 miles. Major Evans transferred R.A.S. Corps.	R.J.O.K.
DOULENS	12th		Squadron marched to LE MARAIS SEC 4 miles.	R.J.O.K.
FRECHENCOURT	13th		Squadron marched to FRECHENCOURT 13 miles. Captain Reid Kerr assumed command.	R.J.O.K.
FRECHENCOURT	14th		A.D. troops built new bridge for cavalry over R. HALLUE & remainder to enable division to cross.	R.J.O.K.
VILLE SUR ANCRE	15th		Squadron marched to VILLE SUR ANCRE. 13 miles. Bivouac camp.	R.J.O.K.
VILLE SUR ANCRE	16th		Squadron carried out improvements to & hedged Cavalry track from Div' Bivouac to MAMETZ.	R.J.O.K.
"	17th		Squadron remained at short notice; Capt Reid Kerr took own look in 2nd Ind. Cav. Tracks running from MAMETZ N of MONTAUBAN, BERNAFAY & TRONES WOODS, between WATERLOT FM & DELVILLE WOOD to GUEUDECOURT	R.J.O.K.
FRICOURT	18th		Squadron marched to FRICOURT where it camped in its Gannow dug outs alongside 2nd Ind. Field Spas. R.E. 'A' Troop worked on forward cavalry track performing linking points. Provided by 1st & 2nd Ind. Dismounted Reinforcements.	R.J.O.K.

1875 W! W593/826 1,000,000 4/15 J.B.C. & A. A.D.S.S./Forms/C. 2118.

WAR DIARY or INTELLIGENCE SUMMARY

Army Form C. 2118

(Erase heading not required.)

Instructions regarding War Diaries and Intelligence Summaries are contained in F.S. Regs., Part II. and the Staff Manual respectively. Title Pages will be prepared in manuscript.

Place	Date	Hour	Summary of Events and Information	Remarks and references to Appendices
FRICOURT	Sept 19	1916	A troop improves Cart Track, C troop bridges along track & B troop makes track passed 300 y⁴⁵ at night.	R.NK.
"	20th		Work on track. Capt Reid Kerr RE on work on 1st Div Track returning from CARNOY to LEUZE Wood.	O.NK.
"	21st		A troop improved & pushes on 1st Div Track with working party. Remainder of 1st I.C.D. dismounted reinforcements.	RdONK.
"	22nd		A & B Troops employed on 1st Div Track with working parties from 1st Div & 1st I.C.D. dismounted reinforcements.	R.NK.
"	23rd		RE dump forms on 1st Div Track S of GUILLEMONT.	ONK.
"	24th		Watering arrangement for 1st I.C.D. finishes at FRICOURT.	ONK.
"	25th		'A' Troop attaches to MHOW BDE which was brought up for active operation against LIGNY TILLOUL. It remained waiting N of BERNAFAY WOOD RE entrain than 'B' Troop attaches to SIALKOT BDE at FRICOURT to support to MHOW BDE.	R.NK.
	26th		Squadron remains at short notice with C Troop ready & in attaches to LUCKNOW BDE	O.NK.
BUSSY LES DAOURS	27th		Squadron marches to bivouac at BUSSY at VILLE bivouac – 15 miles	O.NK.
PICQUIGNY	28th		Squadron marches to billets at PICQUIGNY – 15 miles	R.NK.
FRANCIERES	29th		Squadron marches to billets – 12 miles	R.NK.
CRECY GRANGE	30th		Squadron marches to billets – 16 miles	O.NK.

WAR DIARY.

of

September. 1916.

SERIAL NO. 144.

Confidential
War Diary
of

Field Squadron, 1st Cavalry Division (late 1st C. Div.)

FROM 1st October 1916 TO 30th November
31st October 1916.

WAR DIARY or INTELLIGENCE SUMMARY

Army Form C. 2118

Place	Date	Hour	Summary of Events and Information	Remarks and references to Appendices
CRECY GRANGE	1.10.16.	1916.	Inspections of kits, saddlery, equipment etc.	R.I.P.K.
	2.10.16		Troop training.	R.I.P.K.
	3.10.16		Troop training.	R.I.P.K.
	4.10.16		At New Flagged Divisional Training ground — remainder Troop training	R.I.P.K.
	5.10.16		Routine	R.I.P.K.
	6.10.16		Routine & Brigade Training	R.I.P.K.
	7.10.16		Routine	R.I.P.K.
	8.10.16		Brigade training & Troop Training	M.I.P.K.
	9.10.16		Brigade Training & Troop Training	M.I.P.K.
	10.10.16		Squadron Training	R.I.P.K.
	11.10.16		Squadron mounted sports	R.I.P.K.
	12.10.16		Squadron mounted sports	R.I.P.K.
	13.10.16		Squadron training	R.I.P.K.
	14.10.16		Squadron training	R.I.P.K.
	15.10.16		Routine	M.I.P.K.
MARCHEVILLE	16.10.16		Squadron marches to MARCHEVILLE — 4 miles	R.I.P.K.
	17.10.16		Squadron training exercise in open warfare	R.I.P.K.
	18.10.16		Troop Training	R.I.G.K.
	19.10.16		Troop training. Carpenters employed on work for Signals	R.I.P.K.
	20.10.16		Troop training	R.I.P.K.

WAR DIARY or INTELLIGENCE SUMMARY

Army Form C. 2118

Instructions regarding War Diaries and Intelligence Summaries are contained in F.S. Regs., Part II. and the Staff Manual respectively. Title Pages will be prepared in manuscript.

(Erase heading not required.)

Place	Date	Hour	Summary of Events and Information	Remarks and references to Appendices
MARCHEVILLE	21.10.16	1916.	Exercise. Two sappers sent to Capt Hope to run telephonic extension from Billing Point to Capt Ross Ker. & Telephonic test carried out near new HQ. ST YALERY on S. Can.	Ret. Pk.
	22.10.16	—	Entrenching. Church Parade. Capt Ross Ker went to ST YALERY to deliver over billets at BOISMONT. & Stratton, Pinsate sites Lfm horses of D.A.Q. Advance party went to near BOISMONT.	Ret. Pk. Ret. Pk.
	23.10.16	—	Squadron Training	Q1 Pk.
	24.10.16	—	'C' Troop Marie at Defence W.A.G.S. & Billing at Capt Hope. Exercise.	Q1 Pk.
BOISMONT	25.10.16	—	Squadron marched to BOISMONT 16 miles in 3 hours without in casualty. Horses fed under cover for first time.	Ret Pk.
	26.10.16	—	Detachment started work on 160 yards horse standings at ST YALERY. Carpenters working on Gun piers for Signal Coy. Exercise & settling in to what is imagined to be Winter quarters.	Ret. Pk.
	27.10.16	—	Exercise. Work at ST YALERY continued. Parties of 11 R.D.G. attached for Instrn took at railway.	Q1 Pk.
	28.10.16	—	Exercise. Work at ST YALERY continued. Sergt Moore, c. 11 R.D.G. proceeded to railway.	Q1 Pk.
	29.10.16	—	Exercise. Work at ST YALERY continued. 1 Officer & 17 men of 'C' Trp sent in detachment to Capt Hope, material & procession fuel in town. Exercise. Work at ST YALERY cont.	N. Pk.
	30.10.16	—	Work at ST YALERY cont. Exercise. Carpenters employed on extg trenches. Signal Gun piers.	Q1 Pk.
	31.10.16	—	Exercise. Carpenters employed on extg trenches. Signal Gun piers, & latrine seats.	Q1 Pk.

O.T. 1st Indian Field Squadron R.E.

WAR DIARY.

October 1916.

Army Form C. 2118

WAR DIARY
or
INTELLIGENCE SUMMARY
(Erase heading not required.)

Place	Date	Hour	Summary of Events and Information	Remarks and references to Appendices
BOISMONT	1.11.16		Squadron employed on building stables, huts etc for Division	R/NK
"	2.11.16		ditto	R/NK
"	3.11.16		ditto. Lt Gardner & D Troop went on Detachment for work in	R/NK
"	4.11.16		M40H Bole area	
"	5.11.16		ditto	
"	6.11.16		ditto	
"	7.11.16		ditto	
"	8.11.16		ditto	
"	9.11.16		ditto — Lt Bigg appointed Instructor at Div'l School	
"	10.11.16		ditto	
"	11.11.16		ditto	
"	12.11.16		ditto — 6 Sappers attached to Div'l School	
"	13.11.16		ditto	
"	14.11.16		ditto	
"	15.11.16		ditto	
"	16.11.16		ditto	
"	17.11.16		ditto	
"	18.11.16		ditto	
"	19.11.16		ditto	
"	20.11.16		ditto	NK

Army Form C. 2118

WAR DIARY
or
INTELLIGENCE SUMMARY
(Erase heading not required.)

Instructions regarding War Diaries and Intelligence Summaries are contained in F. S. Regs., Part II. and the Staff Manual respectively. Title Pages will be prepared in manuscript.

Place	Date	Hour	Summary of Events and Information	Remarks and references to Appendices
BOISMONT	21.11.16.		Lt Gardner & 21 O.R. attached to MHOW PIONEER Bn. & 3rd Cav. men.	MJK.
	22.11.16		Lt Graham & 21 O.R. attached to LUCKNOW PIONEER Bn. & proceeded for work in 1st Anzac Corps area.	
	23.11.16		Remainder of Squadron employed on billetting work. Squadron employed on billetting work to Brig. Hordern Temp. Comm. to 4th Field Squadron	MJK
	24.11.16		ditto	
	25.11.16		ditto. Title of Squadron altered to 4th Field Squadron	
	26.11.16		ditto	
	27.11.16		ditto	
	28.11.16		ditto	
	29.11.16		ditto	
	30.11.16		ditto	

M. Gaskin
O.C. 4th Field Squadron R.E.
MJK

WAR DIARY.

November 1916

SERIAL NO. 148.

Confidential

War Diary

of

Field Squadron, R.E., 4th Cavalry Division.

FROM 1st December 1916. TO 31st December 1916.

WAR DIARY or INTELLIGENCE SUMMARY

Army Form C. 2118

4TH FIELD SQUADRON, R.E., 4TH CAVALRY DIVISION.
No. WD/12
Date Dec 1916

Place	Date	Hour	Summary of Events and Information	Remarks and references to Appendices
BOISMONT	1.12.16		Squadron employed on Billeting work.	
	2.12.16		ditto	
	3.12.16		ditto	
	4.12.16		ditto	
	5.12.16		ditto	
	6.12.16		ditto	
	7.12.16		ditto	
	8.12.16		ditto	
	9.12.16		ditto. 2 Sappers sent wounded while on detachment	M.V.K.
	10.12.16		ditto	
	11.12.16		ditto	
	12.12.16		ditto	
	13.12.16		ditto. Lt Gammon & 12 O.R. proceeded with SIALKOT Pioneer Bn to 3rd Corps. 10 O.R. " " " " 1st ANZAC Corps men.	
	14.12.16		ditto. 1st Patrols from 1st ANZAC CORPS returned (Lieuts Graham & Talbot) LUCKNOW " " 2nd Lieutenants & parties from 3rd " returned.	
	15.12.16		ditto	
	16.12.16		ditto	Q.V.K.
	17.12.16		ditto	
	18.12.16		ditto	
	19.12.16		ditto	
	20.12.16		ditto	

WAR DIARY or INTELLIGENCE SUMMARY

Army Form C. 2118

Place	Date	Hour	Summary of Events and Information	Remarks and references to Appendices
BOISMONT	21.12.16		Squadron employed on Billetting work.	
	22.12.16		ditto	
	23.12.16		ditto	
	24.12.16		ditto	
	25.12.16		Christmas Day	
	26.12.16		Squadron employed on billetting work	
	27.12.16		ditto	
	28.12.16		ditto	
	29.12.16		ditto	
	30.12.16		ditto	
	31.12.16		ditto	

A.J. Reed
Major R.E.
O.C. 4th Field Squadron R.E.

WAR DIARY.

4TH
FIELD SQUADRON, R.E.,
4TH CAVALRY DIVISION.

Dec. 1916.

www.ingramcontent.com/pod-product-compliance
Lightning Source LLC
Chambersburg PA
CBHW081551160426
43191CB00011B/1896